The new book of constitutions of the most ancient and honourable fraternity of free and accepted masons Containing their history, charges, regulations, Collected from the book of constitutions published in England, in the year 1738, b

James Anderson

*The new book of constitutions of the most ancient and honourable fraternity of free and accepted masons. Containing their history, charges, regulations, &c. ... Collected from the book of constitutions published in England, in the year 1738, by our worthy brother James Anderson, D.D. For the use of the lodges in Ireland. By Edward Spratt, sec.*
Anderson, James
ESTCID: N040789
Reproduction from Bodleian Library (Oxford)
Originally published as 'The constitutions of the free-masons'. Edward Spratt edited this edition.
Dublin : printed by J. Butler, for the editor, and sold at his house, 1751.
viii,[4],9-172,40p. : plate ; 8°

Eighteenth Century
Collections Online
Print Editions

## Gale ECCO Print Editions

Relive history with *Eighteenth Century Collections Online*, now available in print for the independent historian and collector. This series includes the most significant English-language and foreign-language works printed in Great Britain during the eighteenth century, and is organized in seven different subject areas including literature and language; medicine, science, and technology; and religion and philosophy. The collection also includes thousands of important works from the Americas.

The eighteenth century has been called "The Age of Enlightenment." It was a period of rapid advance in print culture and publishing, in world exploration, and in the rapid growth of science and technology – all of which had a profound impact on the political and cultural landscape. At the end of the century the American Revolution, French Revolution and Industrial Revolution, perhaps three of the most significant events in modern history, set in motion developments that eventually dominated world political, economic, and social life.

In a groundbreaking effort, Gale initiated a revolution of its own: digitization of epic proportions to preserve these invaluable works in the largest online archive of its kind. Contributions from major world libraries constitute over 175,000 original printed works. Scanned images of the actual pages, rather than transcriptions, recreate the works *as they first appeared.*

Now for the first time, these high-quality digital scans of original works are available via print-on-demand, making them readily accessible to libraries, students, independent scholars, and readers of all ages.

For our initial release we have created seven robust collections to form one the world's most comprehensive catalogs of 18$^{th}$ century works.

*Initial Gale ECCO Print Editions collections include:*

### *History and Geography*
Rich in titles on English life and social history, this collection spans the world as it was known to eighteenth-century historians and explorers. Titles include a wealth of travel accounts and diaries, histories of nations from throughout the world, and maps and charts of a world that was still being discovered. Students of the War of American Independence will find fascinating accounts from the British side of conflict.

*Social Science*
Delve into what it was like to live during the eighteenth century by reading the first-hand accounts of everyday people, including city dwellers and farmers, businessmen and bankers, artisans and merchants, artists and their patrons, politicians and their constituents. Original texts make the American, French, and Industrial revolutions vividly contemporary.

*Medicine, Science and Technology*
Medical theory and practice of the 1700s developed rapidly, as is evidenced by the extensive collection, which includes descriptions of diseases, their conditions, and treatments. Books on science and technology, agriculture, military technology, natural philosophy, even cookbooks, are all contained here.

*Literature and Language*
Western literary study flows out of eighteenth-century works by Alexander Pope, Daniel Defoe, Henry Fielding, Frances Burney, Denis Diderot, Johann Gottfried Herder, Johann Wolfgang von Goethe, and others. Experience the birth of the modern novel, or compare the development of language using dictionaries and grammar discourses.

*Religion and Philosophy*
The Age of Enlightenment profoundly enriched religious and philosophical understanding and continues to influence present-day thinking. Works collected here include masterpieces by David Hume, Immanuel Kant, and Jean-Jacques Rousseau, as well as religious sermons and moral debates on the issues of the day, such as the slave trade. The Age of Reason saw conflict between Protestantism and Catholicism transformed into one between faith and logic -- a debate that continues in the twenty-first century.

*Law and Reference*
This collection reveals the history of English common law and Empire law in a vastly changing world of British expansion. Dominating the legal field is the *Commentaries of the Law of England* by Sir William Blackstone, which first appeared in 1765. Reference works such as almanacs and catalogues continue to educate us by revealing the day-to-day workings of society.

*Fine Arts*
The eighteenth-century fascination with Greek and Roman antiquity followed the systematic excavation of the ruins at Pompeii and Herculaneum in southern Italy; and after 1750 a neoclassical style dominated all artistic fields. The titles here trace developments in mostly English-language works on painting, sculpture, architecture, music, theater, and other disciplines. Instructional works on musical instruments, catalogs of art objects, comic operas, and more are also included.

**The BiblioLife Network**

This project was made possible in part by the BiblioLife Network (BLN), a project aimed at addressing some of the huge challenges facing book preservationists around the world. The BLN includes libraries, library networks, archives, subject matter experts, online communities and library service providers. We believe every book ever published should be available as a high-quality print reproduction; printed on-demand anywhere in the world. This insures the ongoing accessibility of the content and helps generate sustainable revenue for the libraries and organizations that work to preserve these important materials.

The following book is in the "public domain" and represents an authentic reproduction of the text as printed by the original publisher. While we have attempted to accurately maintain the integrity of the original work, there are sometimes problems with the original work or the micro-film from which the books were digitized. This can result in minor errors in reproduction. Possible imperfections include missing and blurred pages, poor pictures, markings and other reproduction issues beyond our control. Because this work is culturally important, we have made it available as part of our commitment to protecting, preserving, and promoting the world's literature.

**GUIDE TO FOLD-OUTS MAPS and OVERSIZED IMAGES**

The book you are reading was digitized from microfilm captured over the past thirty to forty years. Years after the creation of the original microfilm, the book was converted to digital files and made available in an online database.

In an online database, page images do not need to conform to the size restrictions found in a printed book. When converting these images back into a printed bound book, the page sizes are standardized in ways that maintain the detail of the original. For large images, such as fold-out maps, the original page image is split into two or more pages

Guidelines used to determine how to split the page image follows:

- Some images are split vertically; large images require vertical and horizontal splits.
- For horizontal splits, the content is split left to right.
- For vertical splits, the content is split from top to bottom.
- For both vertical and horizontal splits, the image is processed from top left to bottom right.

Published by Edward Spratt Secretary to y.e Grand Lodge Dublin

# THE NEW BOOK OF CONSTITUTIONS

OF THE

Most Ancient and Honourable FRATERNITY of FREE and ACCEPTED MASONS.

Containing Their

History, Charges, Regulations, &c.

ALSO

Some RULES necessary to be observed by the *Committee of Charity*, not Published before,

Together with a Choice COLLECTION of MASON's SONGS, POEMS, PROLOGUES, and EPILOGUES.

Published by the ORDER, and with the SANCTION of the

## GRAND-LODGE.

Collected from the

BOOK of CONSTITUTIONS

Published in ENGLAND, in the Year 1738, By our worthy Brother *JAMES ANDERSON*, D.D.

For the USE of the

LODGES in *IRELAND*.

By *EDWARD SPRATT*, Sec.

*And the Light shineth in Darkness, and the Darkness comprehended it not.* St. JOHN chap. i. ver. 5.

DUBLIN:

Printed by J. BUTLER, on *Cork-hill*, For the EDITOR, and Sold at his House in *Nicholas-street*, M,DCC,LI.

*To the Right Worshipfull and Right Honourable The Lord Kingsborough Grand Master of Masons in Ireland for the years 1749 & 1750*

My Lord,

THE early Knowledge in the profound Mysteries of *Free Masonry*, joined to the firm attachment and zealous love expressed by your *Lordship* on all occasions for the *Craft*, since it was first honour'd by your becoming a Member of it, were the chief motives
that

## iv DEDICATION.

that induced the Brethren of the *Grand Lodge* of *Ireland*, to apply for the honour of your *Lordship*'s presiding as their *Grand-Master*: An Office, which your *Lordship* according to the noble and generous manner, truly natural to your self, undertook with such a ready cheerfulness, that it has roused a Spirit of Emulation through the whole Fraternity, who now seem to vye with each other in the Cultivation and Improvement of all that is commendable, making Harmony, Friendship and Brotherly-Love, the Rule by which they square their actions, and the Good of the Community, the Center, to which they all tend.

The constant Visitations, and frequent Lectures on Truth, Justice, and Morality, given by your *Lordship*'s worthy and generous Predecessor in the Chair, revived the then drooping and almost decayed Spirits of the Lodges in this Kingdom. It was he, My Lord, who laid the first foundation

# DEDICATION.

foundation of a Collection, that was to be made for the support of our poor and indigent Brethren; and your *Lordship*, like another Sun, rose with benificent Rays in his room, and according to your usual Humanity and well judg'd Benevolence, assisted in raising such a Superstructure, as will, in all human probability, afford not only a relief to them, but reflect honour on its Supporters and Incouragers.

This single consideration, My Lord, independent of your *Lordship*'s many other personal qualifications, would be alone sufficient to engage, and embolden me with all due Humility, to commit the following sheets to your *Lordship*'s Protection and Patronage, not in Quality of an Author, a task I am every way unequal to, but only as a faithful Editor, and Transcriber of the works of our learned and ingenious brother, *James Anderson*, D. D. dedicated to his Royal Highness

ness *Frederick*, Prince of Wales, at a time, when the Dignity of *Grand-Master* in *England* was supported by the Rt. Hon. the Marquis of *Caernarvon*, and that of the Lodges in *Ireland*, by the Rt. Hon. the then Lord *Mountjoy*, now Earl of *Blessington*, who appointed a select Committee of the *Grand-lodge*, over which he presided, to compare the Customs and Regulations in use here, with those of our Brethren in *England*.

But no essential difference appearing, except in those Rules that tended to the formation of the *Steward's-lodge*, (a thing not practised here,) they were therefore omitted and a Regulation of the other differences that remained, was rather wished for, than establish'd, 'till your *Lordship*'s being chosen to the Chair, when the Lodges becoming more numerous, our Rt. Worshipful Brother *Putland*, your *Lordship*'s Deputy, who makes the Good of the Public in general, and that of the

*Craft*

# DEDICATION. vii

*Craft* in particular, his care, observed with his usual Candour and Prudence, that a publication of these general Regulations was much wanted among the Lodges and Brethren in this Kingdom, and therefore honoured me with his Commands, to prepare them for the Press, which I have done with all the care and exactness I was any way Master of.

And now, My Lord, give me leave to trespass a little further on your *Lordship*'s Patience, and assure you, that as my whole Ambition is not to be useless to the World, though inconsiderable I may appear in it, I have, upon observing that the Committee of Charity had no established Rules to proceed by, ventured to compile for their use, a few drawn from the Usage of our Brethren in *England*, as well as our own Practice here, and as they have received the Approbation of the GRAND-LODGE, who have ordered them to be published with these Regulations,

## viii DEDICATION.

gulations, they will not, I humbly hope, meet with less protection from your *Lordship*, for being compiled by one of the meanest of the Craft, whose sole merit consists in belonging to that Society of which your *Lordship* is a Member, and Patron; and your favour and countenance shall in this, as in every other respect, be most greatfully acknowledged by,

My Lord,

Your Lordship's,

most obliged,

most obedient,

Dublin *March*,
10th 1750.

true, and faithful

*Edward Spratt.*

# SUBSCRIBERS NAMES.

### A
Mr James Anderson,
James Anderson, of Newry,
Mr. William Allen, of Colerain,
Obadiah Askew.
William Archer,

### B
Hon. Brinsley Butler, Esq; G. W.
Capt. George Burston,
Lieut Theodore Bencon,
Geo. Boyde, sen, Esq, D.A.G.
Sir Charles Bingham, Bart.
Capt. James Blaquire,
William Bury, Esq,
Peter Benson, of Derry Esq, 2 Books
Geo. Boyde, jun, Esq;
Mr. Edward Brown,
Dennis Byrne, of Tullow,
Robert Brooks, of L. Derry,
Alex. Buchanon, of Derry, Merchant,
Mark Bellew, of ditto,
Thos Boyle, of ditto,
Alex. Boyde, of ditto,
John Burton, of London,
Nicholas Berwick,
Charles Bellamy,
James Burns,
Rev. Thos. Bowes, of Dundalk
Mr. Richard Brazil,
Henry Betagh, Surgeon,
John Butler, Printer,
Joseph Bromwich,
Thomas Benson,
Mr. Roger O Boylan, of Colrain.
Nicholas Butler, of Corke,
John Baird, of ditto,
George Baxter, of ditto,
Adam Busteed, of ditto,
Richard Barrington, of ditto.
Peter Beasly,

### C
John Cole, of Enniskillen, Esq;
Capt. Hew Craig,
Lieut William Craig,
Major George Crawford,
Michael Cromie, Esq;
Lieut. John Congreve Chillcott,
Stephen Cuppage, of Ballymoney, Esq,
Noble Caldwell, of Derry Gent.
Mr William Carmichal,
John Calder,
Bernard Clarke,
William Cunningham,
Francis Cunningham,
Richard Campbell, of Derry, Merchant,
Samuel Mc.Crea, of Strabane, Philom.
James Clarke, of ditto,
William Canham,
John Crosthwaite,
George Cottingham,
John Constable,
Robert Cochran, of Dundalk,
Westenra Cross, of Newry

Mr.

# SUBSCRIBERS NAMES.

Mr. Andrew Campbell, of Newry, 2 Books
Joshua Carter, Gent.
Mr. Abraham Chatterton, of Corke,
Isaac Clay,
James Cummine,
Callaghan Mc Carty,
Mrs. Ann Cunningham,

### D
Capt. John Donaldson,
James Dover, Gent.
Henry Darcus, of Derry Gent.
Hugh Dunn, Gent.
George Donovan, Gent.
Mr. James Dolan,
James Dellap,
Andrew Dunlap, of Derry, Merchant.
Michael Daly,
Richard Davis, of Corke
William Deering, of ditto,
John Daly, of ditto,

### E
Lieut. Isaac Espinasse,
Charles Eccles, Esq;
Robert Eustace, Esq;
Nathaniel Evans, Esq,
Mr. John Evans,

### F
Major Cecil Forester,
Capt. George Friend,
Capt. Henry Fletcher,
David Fitzgerald, of Corke, Esq; P.D.G.M.M.
Edward Fitzgerald, of ditto, Esq;
Capt. William Farquhar,
Malcoml, Mc.Fadin, of Derry,

Mr. David Fleming,
Andrew Flin, of Colerain,
Thomas Foley,
James Fisher,

### G
Mr. Thomas Gamble, of Derry,
William Gillaspy, of Muff.
Nathan Grant,
Isaac Gladwell,
How Green,
John Gillies,
Serjt John Mc.Glashan,
Mr. Samuel Mc. Gowan, of Newry.
Thomas Gordon,
Ramsay George,

### H
Gorges Edmund Howard, Esq;
Robert Hart, Esq,
Capt. Henry Holmes,
William Hamilton, of Derry, Esq; 3 Books
Richard Haughton, Esq;
Mr. Nathaniel Hunter, of Derry, Merchant,
Edward Harshey, of Muff,
John Henry, of ditto,
Francis Hill, Gent.
Benjamin Higgins, Gent.
Mr. Thomas Harrison,
James Hutchison,
Thomas Hughs,
William Hutchings,
James Harding, of Corke.

### I
Major John Irwin,
George Julian Esq;
Mr. Robert Johnson, of Derry.

Mr.

# SUBSCRIBERS NAMES.

Mr James Jones,
  Samuel Johnson,
  Robert Jones,
  Patrick Johnston,

## K
Right Hon Lord Kingsborough, G.M.
Edward Kelly, Esq,
Edward Kiernan, Gent.
Corporal Kennedy, of Gen. Ligonier's Horse

## L
Boyle Lennox, Esq, G W.
William Lewin, Gent.
Serjant James Levingston,
Mr. John Lewis, of Derry, 6 Books,
John Lyndon,

## M
Hon. Roderick Makenzie, Esq, G W.
Edward Martin, Esq, G T.
Lieut. Col. James Murray,
John Magill, Esq,
Richard Mottley, Esq,
Mr John Murphy, of Muff,
  Adam Mitchell,
  Anthony Malady,
  John Moore,
  Alexander Mathison, Master of the Faulkner Packet-boat.
  Edward Moore,
  Constant Maguire,
  George Mannix, of Corke,
  Thomas Moclar,
  Stephen Miller

## N
Mr. William Nelson, of Derry.
  William Mc.Nemee, of ditto, Merchant.
John Norman,
Dennis Nowlan, of Timolin,
Henry Neiland,
Mrs. Rachell Nowlan,

## O
Capt James OHara,
Mr Robert Orr, of Derry, Merchant 2 Books.
  William Orr, of Strabane, ditto.
Michael OBrien, Gent.

## P
John Putland, Esq, D.G.M.
Capt. Peter Parker,
Francis Palmer, Esq,
Capt. John Pomeroy,
Lieut Cristopher Parker,
Richard Poole Gent.
Mr. Thomas Price, jun. of Derry, Merchant.
  James Pinkerton, of ditto.
  James Parkinson,
  Francis Parvisole,
  Sam. Pettycrew, of Newry.
  Samuel Payne, of Corke,
  Peter Parks, of ditto,
  William Parks, of ditto,
  John Peirle, of ditto,

## Q
Mr. Patrick Quig, of Derry,
  William Quinn, of Muff,
    Major

# SUBSCRIBERS NAMES.

### R
Major Henry Richardson,
Anthony Rellhan, Esq, M D
Mr James Ramage, of Derry, Merchant.
John Reames, of ditto,
Thomas Ramage, of Muff,
John Reabby
David Ryan, of Moylabby,
Richard Robbins,
John Riordar,
Lawrence Rochford, of Corke
Henry Rugg, of ditto,

### S
Right Hon. Lord George Sackville, Principal Secretary to His Grace the Duke of Dorset, Lord Lieutenant of Ireland, G M.
Right Hon Lord Southwell,
Hon. Thomas Southwell, Esq, D. G. M
Capt. Francis Smyth,
Mr. Richard St. Leger, of Derry,
John Sherky, of ditto,
Ben. Stokes,
Patrick Supple, of Cromlin
John Steward,
John Sherrar,
Ephraim Smallwood,
Thomas Shephard,
Mr Ellory Sweet,
John Scott, of Corke,
Edward Scott, of ditto,
Richard Sharp,
William Savill,
John Stordy,
Nathaniel Anthony Smith,

### T
Right Hon Earl of Tyrone,
Right Hon Lord Tullamoore,
Lieut Col John Tovie,
Lieut John Travers,
Mr William Tradenick, of Derry Merchant,
James Tiernan,
John Tomlinson,
Gray Townsend,
James Turner,

### W
Sir Marmaduke Wyvill, Bart. Post Master General of Ireland G M.
Capt Edward Windus,
George Winstanly, Esq;
Mr Richard Woodward,
George Williamson,
William Walsh,
John Wrightson,
John White, of Newry,
Samuel West, of Corke,
Robert West,

### Z
Mr. Mark Zouch, Gent.

# THE NEW BOOK

OF

# CONSTITUTIONS

OF THE

Most *Ancient* and *Honourable* FRATERNITY of

# FREE and ACCEPTED MASONS.

The History of *Masonry* from the Creation throughout the known Earth; 'till true old *Architecture* was demolish'd by the *Goths*, and at last revived in *Italy*.

## CHAP. I.

From the Creation to *Grand Master* NIMROD.

THE almighty Architect and *Grand Master* of the Universe having created all things very good, and according to Geometry, last of all formed *Adam* after his own Image, ingraving on his Heart the said noble Science; which *Adam* soon discover'd by Surveying his earthly Paradise, and the Fa-

B  brication

brication of the Arbour or Silvan Lodgment that God had prepared for him, a well propotioned and convenient place of Shelter from Heat, and of Retirement, Rest, and Repast, after his wholesome Labour in cultivating his Garden of Delights, and the first Temple or place of Worship, agreeable to his Original, perfect and innocent State.

    A. M. Or Year of the World ——— 1 ⎫
 * B. C. Or before the Christian Æra. 4003 ⎭

But tho' by Sin *Adam* fell from his original happy State, and was expell'd from his lovely Arbour and Earthly Paradise into the wide World, he still retain'd great Knowledge, especially in *Geometry*; and its principles

---

  * The first Christians computed their times as the Nations among whom they lived till A. D. 532, when *Dionysius Exiguus*, a Roman Abbot taught them first to compute from the Birth of Christ But he lost 4 Years, or began the Christian Æra 4 Years later than just. Therefore, tho' according to the Hebrew Chronoligy of the Old Testament and other good Vouchers, Christ was truly Born in some Month of the year of the World or A M. 4000 yet these 4 years added make ——— ——— 4004. ⎫
Not before the Birth of Christ, but before the Christian
   Æra, viz. ——— ——— — 1750 ⎭
For the true Anno Domini or year after Christ's Birth is  1754
But the *Masons* being used to compute by the Vulgar Anno ⎫ 1750
  Domini or Christian Æra. ⎭
And adding to it not 4004 as it ought, but the strict ⎫ 4000
  years before Christ's Birth, viz. ⎭
They usually call this the year of *Masonry*    5750
Instead of the Accurate year    5754
And we must keep to the Vulgar Computation.
  These Letters A. M. signify Anno Mundi or year of the World: And here B. C. is not before Christ, but before the Christian Æra.
  The A. M. or Anno Mundi is the same follow'd by *Usher* and *Prideaux* &c.

                                 remaining

remaining in the Hearts of his Offspring, have in process of time been drawn forth in a convenient method of Propositions, according to the laws of Proportion taken from Mechanism: And as the Mechanical Arts gave occasion to the Learned to reduce the Elements of *Geometry* into Method; so this noble Science, thus reduc'd and methodized, is now the Foundation of all those Arts (especially of Architecture) and the Rule by which they are conducted and finish'd.

*Adam*, when expell'd, resided in the most convenient natural abodes of the land of *Eden*, where he could best be shelter'd from Colds and Heats, from Winds, Rains, and Tempests, and from wild Beasts; till his Sons grew up to form a *Lodge*, whom he taught *Geometry* and the great use of it in Architecture, without which the Children of Men must have liv'd like Brutes in Woods, Dens, and Caves, &c. or at best in poor Hutts of Mud, or Arbours made of Branches of Trees, &c.

Thus *Kain* when expell'd * with his Family and adherents from *Adam*'s Altars, built forthwith a strong City, and     * A. M. 130.
call'd it *Dedicate*, or *Consecrate*, after the Name of his eldest Son *Enoch*; whose Race follow'd the Example, improving the Arts and Sciences of their Patriarch: For *Tubal Kain* wrought in Metals, *Jubal* elevated Musick, and *Jabal* extended his Tents.

Nor was his Brother *Seth* less instructed, the Patriarch of the other half of Mankind, who transmitted *Geometry* and *Masonry* to his late Posterity, who were the better skill'd by *Adam*'s living among them till he Died. A. M. 930.

*Adam* was succeeded in the Grand Direction of the *Craft* by *Seth, Enosh, Kainan, Mahalaleel,* and *Jared,* whose Son Godly *Enoch* died not, but was Translated alive,

alive, Soul and Body, into Heaven, aged 365 Years.

\* A. M. 130.  \* He was expert and bright both in the Science and the Art, and being a Prophet, he foretold the Destruction of the Earth for Sin, first by Water, and afterwards by Fire: Therefore *Enoch* erected two large Pillars, § the one of Stone and the other of Brick, whereon he Engraved the Abridgments of the Arts and Sciences, particularly *Gometry* and *Masonry*.

*Jared* lived after his Son *Enoch* 435 years, and Died, aged 962. A. M. 1422, the oldest Man except his Grandson.

*Methuselah* the Son of *Enoch*, who succeeded *Jared*; but *Methuselah* ruled not long: For the Immoral Corruption universally prevailing,

*Methuselah*, with his Son *Lamech* and Grandson *Noah* retired from the corrupt World, and in their own peculiar Families preserved the good old Religion of the promised Messiah, pure, and also the Royal Art, till the Flood: For *Lamech* died only five years before the Flood, and *Methuselah* died a few years before it, Aged 969 years: And so he could well Communicate the Traditions of his learned Progenitors to *Noah*'s three Sons; for *Japhet* lived with him 100 years. *Shem* 98, and *Ham* 96.

At last, when the World's Destruction drew nigh, God commanded *Noah* to build the great Ark or Floating Castle, and his three Sons assisted like a *Deputy*, and two *Wardens*: That edifice tho' of Wood only, was fabricated by *Geometry*, as nicely as any Stone Building (like true Ship-Building to this Day) a Curi-

---

§ Some call them Seth's Pillars, but the old *Masons* always call'd them Enoch's Pillars, and firmly believ'd this Tradition: Nay Josephus (Book 1. Chap. 2.) affirms the Stone Pillar still remain'd in Syria to his time.

ous and large piece of Architecture, and finish'd when *Noah* enter'd into his 600 year; aboard which he and his three Sons and their four Wives passed, and having received the Cargo of Animals by God's Direction they were saved in the Ark,
while the rest perished in the Flood *    * A. M. 1656
for their Immorality and unbelief.    B. C. 2348

And so from these *Masons*, or four Grand-Officers, the whole present Race of Mankind are descended.

After the Flood, *Noah* and his three Sons, having preserved the Knowledge of the Arts and Sciences, Communicated it to their growing Offspring, who were all of one Language and Speech, and it came to pass, § as they Journied from the
East (the plains of Mount Ararat    § *Gen.* XI. 1, 2.
where the Ark rested) towards the
West, they found a Plain in the Land of *Shinar*, and dwelt there together, as *Noachidæ*, † or Sons of *Noah*: And when *Peleg* was born there to *Heber*, after the Flood 101 years, Father *Noah* partition'd the Earth, ordering them to disperse and take Possession; but from a fear of the ill Consequences of Separation, they Resolved to keep together.

---

† The first name of *Masons*, according to some old Traditions.

CHAP.

## CHAP. II.

## From *Nimrod*, to *Grand-Master* SOLOMON.

NIMROD* the Son of *Cush*, the eldest Son of *Ham*, was at the Head of those that would not Disperse; or if they must separate, they resolv'd to Transmit their Memorial Illustrious to all future Ages; and so employ'd themselves under Grand-Master *Nimrod*, in the large and fertile vale of *Shinar* along the banks of the *Tygris*, in Building a great and stately Tower and City, the largest work that ever the World saw (describ'd by various Authors) and soon fill'd the Vale with splended Edifices; but they over-built it, and knew not when to desist, 'till their vanity provoked their Maker to confound their grand Design, by confounding their Lip or Speech. Hence the City was called *Babel Confusion*.

§ A. M. 1810　　Thus they were forced to disperse about 53 years after they began to
B. C. 2194　　Build, or after the Flood 154 years,
　　　　　　§ when, the general Migration from *Shinar* commenced.

They went off at various times, and travelled North, South, East and West, with their mighty skill, and found the good use of it, in setling their Colonies.

---

* *Nimrod* signifies a Rebel, the name that the Israelites gave him; but his friends call'd him *Belus* Lord.

But *Nimrod* went forth no farther than into the Land of *Assyria*, and founded the first great Empire at his Capital *Niniveh*, where he long Reign'd; and under him flourished many learned Mathematicians, whose Successors were long afterwards call'd Chaldees and Magians: And though many of them turned Image-Worshipers, yet even that Idolatry occasion'd an Improvement in the arts of designing: * for *Ninus* King of *Niniveh* or *Assyria* order'd his best Artists to frame the Statue of *Baal*, that was worshipped in a Gorgeous Temple.

From *Shinar*, the Science and the Art were carried to the distant parts of the Earth, notwithstanding the confusion of Dialects: That indeed gave rise to the *Masons* Faculty and universal Practice of conversing without speaking, and of knowing each other by Signs and Tokens († which they settled upon the dispersion or Migration, in case any of them should meet in distant parts, who had been before in *Shinar*) but it hindred not the propagation of *Masonry*, which was cultivated by all the first Nations; 'till the negligence of their Chiefs and their horrid Wars, made them turn Ignorant, and lose their original skill in Arts and Sciences.

Thus the Earth was again Planted and Replenish'd with *Masons*, from the Vale of *Shinar*, whose various Improvements we shall trace.

*Mitzraim* or *Menes*, the second Son of *Ham*, led his Colony from *Shinar* to *Egypt* (which is Mitzraim in Hebrew, a dual word, signifying both *Egypts*, Upper and Lower) after the Flood 160 years, and after the Confusion 6 years, A. M. 1816, where they pre-

---

\* Viz. Architecture, Sculpture, Statuary, Plastering and Painting.
† This old Tradition is believ'd firmly by the old Fraternity.

serv'd

ferved their original fkill, and much cultivated the Art: For antient Hiftory informs us of the Early fine Tafte of the *Egyptians*, their many magnificent Edefices and great Cities, as *Memphis*, *Heliopolis*, *Thebes* with 100 Gates, &c. befides their Palaces and Sepulchres, their Obelifks and Statues, the Coloffal Statue of *Sphinx*, whofe Head was 120 Foot round, and their famous Pyramids, the § greateft being reckoned the firft or earlieft of the feven Wonders of Art after the General Migration.

* Diod. Sicul. Lib. 1.

The *Egyptians* excell'd all Nations in their amazing Labyrinths, one of them cover'd the ground of a whole Province, containing many fine Palaces and 100 Temples, difpofed in its feveral quarters and divifions, adorned with Columns of the beft Porphyre, and the accurate Statues of their Gods and Princes; which Labyrinth the *Greeks*, long afterwards endeavoured to imitate, but never arrived at its Extenfion and Sublime.

The Succeffors of *Mitzraim* (who ftiled themfelves the Sons of antient Kings) Encourag'd the Royal Art down to the laft of the Race, the learned King *Amafis*. See Chap. IV.

But Hiftory fails us in the South and Weft of *Africa*. Nor have we any juft Accounts of the fair and Gallant Pofterity of *Noah*'s eldeft Son *Japhet*, that firft replenifh'd vaft old *Scythia*, from *Norway* Eaftward to *America*; nor of the *Japhetites* in *Greece* and *Italy*,

---

§ Some fay it was built of Marble Stones brought from the Quarries of Arabia; for there is no Veftige of a Quarry near it. Others call them Artificial Stones made on the fpot, moft of them 30 Foot long. The Pile at bottom was 700 Foot fquare, and 481 Foot high; but others make it much higher: And in rearing it 360,000 *Mafons* were employ'd for 20 years, as if all the People had join'd in the Grand Defign.

*Germany*,

*Germany*, *Gaul* and *Britain*, &c. 'till their Original Skill was lost: But, no doubt, they were good Architects at their first Migration from *Shinar*.

*Shem*, the second Son of *Noah*, remain'd at *Ur* of the *Chaldees* in *Shinar*, with his Father and Great Grandson *Heber*, where they liv'd private, and died in Peace; but *Shem*'s Off-spring travell'd into the South and East of great *Asia*, viz. *Elam*, *Ashur*, *Arphaxad*, *Lud* and *Aram*, with *Sala* the Father of *Heber*, and their Offspring propogated the Science and Art as far as *China* and *Japan*. while *Noah*, *Shem*, and *Heber*, diverted themselves at *Ur*, in Mathematical Studies, teaching *Peleg* the Father of *Rehu*, Father of *Serug*, Father of *Nachor*, Father of *Terah*, Father of *Abram*, a learned Race of Mathematicians and Geometricians *.

Thus *Abram*, born two Years after the death of *Noah*, § had learned well the Science and the Art, before the God of Glory call'd him to travel from *Ur* of the *Chaldees*, and to live a Peregrine, not in Stone and Brick but in Tents erected also by Geometry. So travelling with his Family and Flocks through *Mesopotamia*, he pitched at *Charran*, † where old *Terah* in five Years Died, and then *Abram* Aged 75 Years, Travell'd into the Land of the *Canaanites* ‖ but a Famine soon forced him down to *Egypt*; and returning next Year, he began to Communicate his great Skill to the chief of the *Canaanites*, for which they Honour'd him as a Prince.

§ A. M. 2008.

† A. M. 2078.

‖ A. M. 2083.
B. C. 1921.

*Abram* Transmitted his Geometry to all his Offspring; *Isaac* did the same to his two Sons, and *Jacob*

---

* The old Constitutions affirm this strongly, and Expatiate on *Abram*'s great Skill in Geometry, and of his teaching it to many Scholars, tho' all the Sons of the Free born only.

well instructed his Family; while his Son *Joseph* was *Grand-Master* of the *Egyptian Masons*, and Employ'd them in Building many Granaries and Store-Cities throughout the Land of *Egypt*, before the descent of *Jacob* and his Family.

Indeed this peculiar Nation were chiefly conversant in Tents and Flocks and Military skill, for about 350 Years after *Abram* came to *Canaan*, 'till their Persecution began in *Egypt*, about 80 Years before the *Exodus* of *Moses*: But then the *Egyptians* having spoil'd and enslaved the *Hebrews*, trained them up in *Masonry* of Stone and Brick, and made them Build two Strong and Stately Cities for the Royal Treasures, *Pithom* and *Raamses*. Thus the Divine Wisdom appeared in permitting them to be thus Employ'd before they possess'd the Promised Land, then abounding with fine Architecture.

At length, after *Abram* left *Charran* 430 Years, *Moses* marched out of *Egypt* * at the Head of 600,000 Hebrew Males, Marshall'd in due form; for whose sake God divided the Red Sea, to let them pass through, and Drowned *Pharoah* and the *Egyptians* that pursued them.

* A. M. 2513.
B. C. 1491.

While Marching through *Arabia* to *Canaan*, God was pleased to Inspire their *Grand-Master Moses*, * *Joshua* his Deputy, and *Aholiab* and *Bazaleel* *Grand Wardens*, with Wisdom of Heart, and so next Year they raised the curious *Tabernacle* or Tent (where the Divine *Shechinah* Resided, and the Holy Ark or Chest, the Simbole of God's presence) which though not of Stone or Brick, was fram'd by Geometry, a most Beautiful piece of true Symmetrical Architecture, according to the Pattern that God Discovered to *Moses*

* *Exod.* xxxii. 6.

on

on Mount *Sinai*, and it was afterwards the Model of *Solomon*'s Temple.

*Moses* being well skill'd in all the *Egyptian* Learning, and also Divinely Inspired, Excell'd all *Grand-Masters* before him, and ordered the more skilful to meet him, as in a *Grand-Lodge*, near the Tabernacle in the Passover-Week, and gave them wise Charges, Regulations, &c. though we wish they had been more Distinctly Transmitted by Oral Tradition. But of this enough. When *Moses* King of *Jessurun* Died, A. M. 2553.

*Joshua* succeeded in the Direction, with *Kaleb* as Deputy, and *Eleazer* with his Son *Phineas* as *Grand-Wardens*, he Marshall'd his *Ifrealites*, and led them over the *Jordan* (which God made Dry for their March) into the promised Land: And *Joshua* soon found the *Canaanites* had so regularly fortified their great Cities and Passes, that without the Intervention of his *El Shaddai*, in behalf of his peculiar, they were Impregnable and Invincible.

*Joshua* having finish'd his Wars in 6 Years A. M. 2559 fixed the Tabernacle at *Shiloh* in *Ephraim*, according to the Chiefs of *Israel*, not only to serve *Jehovah* their God, and to Cultivate the Land, but also to carry on the Grand Design of Architecture in the best Mosaic Stile.

Indeed the *Ifrealites*, refin'd in Cities and Mansions, having many expert Artists in every Tribe that met in *Lodges* or *Societies* for that purpose, except, when for their Sins they came under Servitude; but their Occasional Princes, call'd Judges and Saviours, revived the Mosaic Stile along with Liberty and the Mosaic Constitution, and only came short of the *Phœnicians* and *Canaanites* in sacred Architecture of Stone; for the *Phœnicians* had many Temples for their Gods: And yet the one Temple or Tabernacle of the one True God at *Shiloh*, Exceeded them all in Wisdom and Beauty, though not in Strength and Dimensions.

Mean while, in Lesser *Asia*, about ten Years before the *Exodus* of *Moses*, *Troy* was founded and stood Sublime till destroy'd by the *Emulous Greeks*, about the 12th Year of *Tolah* Judge of *Israel*. A. M. 2819.

And soon after the *Exodus*, the famous Temple of *Jupiter Hammon* in *Libian Africa* was Erected, that stood till demolish'd by the first Christians in those parts.

The *Sidonians* also, expert Artists, first Built *Tyre*, and a Colony of *Tyrians* first Built *Carthage*; while the Greeks were obscure, and the Romans Existed not yet.

But the *Phænicians* improved their Sacred Architecture, for we read of the Temple of *Dagon* in *Gaza*, very Magnificent and Capacious of 3000 People under its Roof, that was artfully supported only by two Columns, not too big to be grasp'd in the Arms of *Samson*, who tugg'd them down; and the large Roof, like a Burst of Thunder, fell upon the Lords and Ladies, the Priests and People of the *Philistines*; nay *Samson* was also intangled in the same Death that he drew upon his Enemies for the Loss of Liberty and Eyes. After the *Exodous* of *Moses* 379. Before the Temple of *Solomon* 101.[*]

*Abibalus*, King of *Tyre*, Beautified that City; and so did his Son King *Hiram* who Built three Stately Temples to *Jupiter*, *Hercules*, and *Astarte*, the *Tyrian*

---

[*] The Tradition of old *Masons* is, that a learned *Phænician* call'd *Sanconiathon* was the Architect or *Grand Master*, of this curious Temple. and that *Samson* had been too Credulous and Effeminate in revealing his secrets to his Wife, who betray'd him into the Hands of the *Philistines*, for which he is not numbered among the Antient *Masons*. But no more of this.

Gods, and assisted *David* King of *Israel* in Erecting his Palace of Cedar.

Many Monuments of the Primitive Architecture are obscured with Fables, for the True old Histories are lost, or worn out by the Teeth of Time, and also the Oral Tradition is darkened by the Blending of the Nations.

---

# CHAP. III.

## From *Solomon* to *Grand-Master* CYRUS.

BUT the most magnificent Structures of *Gaza*, *Gath*, and *Askelon*, *Jebusi* and *Hebron*, *Tyre* and *Sidon*, *Ægypt* and *Assyria*, &c. were not comparable to the ETERNAL's Temple at *Jerusalem*, built by that wisest meer Man and most glorious King of *Israel*, *Solomon*, (the Son of *David*, who was denied that Honour for being a Man of Blood) the Prince of Peace and Architecture, the Grand Master Mason of his Day, who performed all by divine Direction, and without the Noise of Tools; all the Stones, Timbers and Foundings, being brought ready cut, fram'd and polish'd to *Jerusalem*.

It

It was founded in the fourth Year of *Solomon*, on the second Day of the second Month of the Year after the Exodus ——— ——— 480

\* A. M 2993
B. C. 1011

and *Solomon* \* employ'd about it, tho' not all upon it, the following Number of Operators viz.

See 1 Kings v. 16. 18.
2 Chron. ii. 18.

1. *Harodim*, Rulers or Provosts, call'd also *Menatchim*, Overseers and Comforters of the People in working, that were expert Master Masons in number    3,600

2 *Ghiblim*, Stone-cutters and Sculptors, and *Ish Chotzeb*, Men of hewing, and *Bonai* Setters, Layers or Builders, or bright Fellow-Crafts, in Number ——— ——— 80,000

3. The levy of Assistants under the noble *Adoniram* who was junior Grand-Warden,    30,000

In all Free-Masons ——— ——— 113,600

Besides the Labourers called *Ish Sabal*, or Men of Burden, who were of the Remains of the old *Canaanites*, and being Bond-men, are not to be reckoned among Masons.    70,000

In all ——— 183,600

*Solomon* had the Labourers of his own; but was greatly oblig'd to *Hiram* King of *Tyre* for many of the *Ghiblim* and *Bonai*, who lent him his best Artists, and sent him the Firs and Cedars of *Lebanon*: But above all he sent him his Namesake *Hiram Abbif*, the most accomplish'd

---

\* In 2 Chron. ii. 13. *Hiram* King of *Tyre* (called there *Huram* in his Letter to King *Solomon*, says, I have sent a cunning Man *Ie Huram Abbi*; which is not to be translated like the vulgar Greek

( 23 )

accomplish'd Designer and Operator upon Earth, who in *Solomon*'s absence fill'd the Chair as Deputy *Grand-Master*, and in his Presence was the Senior *Grand-Warden*, or principal Surveyor and Master of the Work.

*Solomon*

---

Greek and Latin, *Huram my Father*; for his description verse 14th refutes it, and the Words import only *Huram, of my Father's,* the chief Master Mason of my Father *Abibalus.* Yet some think that King *Hiram* might call the Architect *Huram* his Father, as learned and wise Men were wont to be call'd by Royal Patrons in the old times: Thus *Joseph* was call'd *Abreck,* or the King's Father; and this same *Hiram* the Architect is called *Solomon*'s Father 2. Chron iv. 6.

*Gnasah Churam Abbif la Melech Shelomoh.*
Did *Hiram* his Father make to king *Solomon.*

But the Difficulty is over at once by allowing the Word *Abbif* to be the Sirname of *Hiram* the Artist, call'd above, *Hiram Abbi*, and here call'd *Huram Abbif*, as in the Lodge he is call'd *Hiram Abbif*, to distinguish him from King *Hiram*. For this Reading makes the sense plain and compleat, viz. That *Hiram* King of *Tyre* sent to King *Solomon* the cunning Workman call'd *Hiram Abbif.*

He is describ'd in two places, 1 Kings vii. 13, 14, 15 and 2 Chron ii 13, 14 in the first he is call'd a Widow's Son of the Tribe of *Naphtali*, and in the other, he is called the Son of a Woman of the Daughters of *Dan*, but in both, that his Father was a Man of *Tyre*. That is, she was of the Daughters of the City of *Dan*, in the Tribe of *Naphtali*, and is call'd a Widow of *Naphtali*, as her Husband was a *Naphtalite*, for he is not call'd a *Tyrian* by descent, but a Man of *Tyre* by Habitation, as *Obed-Edom* the Levite is called a *Gittite*, and the Apostle *Paul* a Man of *Tarsus.*

But tho' *Hiram Abbif* had been a *Tyrian* by Blood, that derogates not from his vast Capacity; for the *Tyrians* were now the best Artificers, by the encouragement of King *Hiram*: and those Texts Testify that God had endued this *Hiram Abbif* with Wisdom Understanding, and mechanical Cunning to perform every thing that *Solomon* required, not only in building the Temple with all

*Solomon* [*] Partitioned the *Fellow-Crafts* into certain *Lodges*, with a *Master* and *Wardens* in Each; that they might receive Commands in a regular manner, might take care of their Tools and Jewels, might be regularly paid every Week, and be duly Fed and Cloathed, &c. and the *Fellow-Crafts* took care of their Succession by Educating enter'd Prentices.

Thus a solid Foundation was laid, of perfect Harmony among the Brotherhood, the *Lodge* was strongly Cemented with Love and Friendship, every Brother was duly taught Secrecy and Prudence, Morality and good Fellowship, each knew his peculiar Business, and the Grand Design was Vigorously pursued at a Prodigious Expence.

For besides King *David*'s vast Preparations, his Richer Son *Solomon*, and all the wealthy *Israelites*, nay even the Princes of the Neighbouring Gentiles, largely contributed towards it, in Gold, Silver and rich Jewels, that amounted to a Sum almost incredible: But all was needful:

For the Wall round it was in Compass 7700 Foot, the Materials were the best that the Earth produced, and no Structure was ever like it for Exactly propotion'd and Beautiful Dimensions, from the most Magnificent on the East, to the Glorious SANCTUM SANCTORUM on the West, with numerous Apartments, pleasant and convenient Chambers and Lodgings for the Kings

---

its costly Magnificence, but also in Founding, fashioning and framing all the holy Utensils thereof, according to Geometry, and to find out every Device that should be put to him. And the Scripture assures us that he fully maintain'd his Character in far larger Works than those of *Aholiab* and *Bazaleel*, for which he will be honoured in the Lodges 'till the End of Time.

[*] According to the Traditions of Old *Masons*, who talk much of these things.

and

and Princes, the *Sanhedrin*, the Priests and Levites of *Israel*, and the outer Court of the Gentiles too, it being an House of Prayer for all Nations, and capable of receiving in all its Courts and Apartments together about 300,000 People.

It was adorned with 1453 Columns of Parian Marble twisted, or sculptured or fluted, with twice as many Pillasters, both having exquisite Capitals or Chapiters of several different noble Orders, and about 2246 Windows, besides those in the curious Pavement; and it was lined with massy Gold, set with Innumerable Diamonds and other precious Stones, in the most Harmonious, Beautiful and Costly Decoration: Tho' much more might be said, if it had not been so often delineated, Particularly by *Villalpandus*.

So that its Prospect highly Transcended all that we are now Capable to Imagine, and has ever been esteemed the finest piece of *Masonry* upon Earth, before or since, the second and chief of the seven Wonders of Art, since the general Migration from *Shinar*.

It was finish'd in the short Space of seven Years and six Months, * to the amazement of all the World, when the Cape-Stone was Celebrated by the Fraternity with great Joy. But their Joy was soon Interrupted by the sudden Death of their dear Master *Hiram Abbif*, whom they decently Interred in the *Lodge* near the Temple, according to antient usage.

\* A. M. 3000
B. C. 1004

After *Hiram Abbif* was mourned for, the Tabernacle of *Moses* and his Holy Reliques being Lodged in the Temple, *Solomon* in a general Assembly Dedicated or Consecrated it by Solemn Prayer and costly Sacrafices past Number, with the finest Music, Vocal and Instrumental, praising JEHOVAH, upon fixing the *Holy Ark* in its proper Place, between the *Cherubims*; when JEHOVAH filled his own Temple with a Cloud of Glory!

But leaving what must not, and indeed cannot be committed to Writing, we may certainly affirm, that however Ambitious and Emulous the Gentiles were in improving the Royal Art, it was never perfected till the Building of this Gorgeous House of God, fit for the special Refulgence of his Glory upon Earth, where he dwelt between the *Cherubims* on the mercy Seat above the Ark, and from thence gave his Frequent Oraculous Responces. This glorious Edifice attracted soon the inquisitive Connisseurs of all Nations to travel and spend some time at *Jerusalem*, to survey its peculiar Excellencies, as much as was allow'd to the *Gentiles*; and they soon discovered that all the World, with their joynt skill, came far short of the *Israelites* in the Wisdom, Strength and Beauty of Architecture; when the wise King *Solomon* was *Grand-Master* of all *Masons* at *Jerusalem*, and the Learned King *Hiram* * was *Grand-Master* at *Tyre*, and Inspired *Hiram Abbif*, had been Master of Work; when true compleat *Masonry* was under the Immediate care and Direction of Heaven; when the Noble and the Wise thought it their Honour to be the Associates of the Ingenious *Craftsmen* in their well formed *Lodges*; and so the Temple of JEHOVAH, the one True God, became the just Wonder of all Travellers, by which, as by the most perfect Pattern, they resolved to Correct the Architecture of their own Countries upon their return.

---

* The Tradition is, that King *Hiram* had been *Grand-Master* of all *Masons*, but when the Temple was finish'd *Hiram* came to Survey it before its Consecration, and to Commune with *Solomon* about Wisdom and Art, and finding the Great Architect of the Universe, had inspired *Solomon* above all mortal Men, *Hiram* very readily veilded the pre-eminence to *Solomon Jedidiah*, the Beloved of God.

*Solomon* next Employ'd the Fraternity in carrying on his other Works, *viz.* His two Palaces at *Jerusalem* for himself and his Queen.———The stately Hall of Judicature with his Ivory throne and Golden Lyons. ———Millo, or the Royal Exchange, made by filling up the great Gulph, between Mount *Moriah* and Mount *Zion*, with strong Arches, upon which many Beautiful Piazzas were Erected with lofty Colionading on each side, and between the Columns a spacious walk from *Zion-Castle* to the *Temple*, where Men of Business met———The House of the *Forrest* of *Lebannon* built upon four Rows of Cedar-Pillars, his Summer House to retire from the Heat of Business, with a *Watch-Tower*, that look'd to the Road to *Damascus* ———Several Cities on the Road between *Jerusalem* and *Lebanon*. Many Store-Houses *West* of the *Jordan*, and several Store-Cities East of that River well fortified,———And the City *Tadmor* (call'd afterwards by the Greeks *Palmyra*) with a splendid Palace in it, the Glorious ruins of which are seen by Travellers to this Day.

All these and many more costly Buildings were finish'd in the short space of 13 Years after the Temple, by the care of 550 *Harodim* and *Menatzchim*: For *Masonry* was carried on throughout all his Dominions, and many particular *Lodges* were Constituted under *Grand Master Solomon*, who annually assembled the *Grand-Lodge* at *Jerusalem*, for Transmitting their Affairs to Posterity: Tho' still the loss of *Hiram Abbif* was Lamented.

Indeed this Wise *Grand-Master Solomon*, shew'd the imperfection of Human Nature, even at its Height of Excellency, by loving too much many strange Women, who turn'd him from the true Religion: But our Business with him is only as a *Mason*; for even during his Idolatry he built some curious Temples to

*Chemosh,*

*Chemosh*, *Molech* and *Ashtaroth*, the Gods of his Concubines, till about three Years before he died, when he Composed his Penitential Song, the Ecclesiastes; and fix'd the true Motto on all Earthly Glory, viz. VANITY OF VANITIES, ALL IS VANITY, *without the fear of God and the keeping of his Commands, which is the whole Duty of Man!* \* And died Aged 58 Years.

\* A. M. 3029.    Many of *Solomon*'s *Masons* before
B. C. 975.    he died began to Travel, and carry'd with them the High Taste of Architecture, with the Secrets of the Fraternity, into *Syria*, Lesser *Asia*, *Mesopotamia*, *Scythia*, *Assyria*, *Chaldæa*, *Media*, *Bactria*, *India*, *Persia*, *Arabia*, *Egypt*, and other parts of Great *Asia* and *Africa*; also into *Europe*, no doubt, tho' we have no History to assure us yet of the Transactions of *Greece* and *Italy*: But the Tradition is, that they travell'd to *Hercules* Pillars on the West, and to *China* on the East: And the old Constitutions affirm, that one called *Ninus*, who had been at the Building of *Solomon*'s Temple, brought the refined knowledge of the Science and the Art into *Germany* and *Gaul*.

In many places, being highly Esteem'd, they obtained special Priviledges; and because they taught their Liberal art only to the Free born, they were call'd *Free-Masons*; constituting *Lodges* in the places where they Built their Stately Piles, by the Encouragement of the Great and Wealthy, who soon requested to be accepted as Members of the *Lodge* and Brethren of the *Craft*; till by Merit those *Free and Accepted Masons*, came to be *Masters* and *Wardens*.

Nay Kings, Princes and Potentates became *Grand-Masters*, each in his own Dominion, in Imitation of King *Solomon*, whose Memory, as a *Mason* has been duly Worship'd, and will be, 'till Architecture shall be consumed in the general Conflagration; for he never

can

can be Rivall'd but by one equally Inspired from above.

After *Solomon*'s death, the Partition of his Empire into the Kingdoms of *Israel* and *Judah*, did not demolish the *Lodges*: For in *Israel*, King *Jeroboam* erected the two curious Statues of the Golden Calves at *Dan* and *Bethel*, with Temples for their Worship; King *Baasha* built *Tirzah* for his Palace, and King *Omri* built *Samaria* for his Capital; where his Son King *Achab* built a large and Sumptuous Temple for his Idol *Baal* (afterwards destroy'd by King *Jehu*) and a Palace of *Ivory*, besides many Castles and fenced Cities.

But *Solomon*'s Royal race, the King's of *Judah*, succeeded him also in the *Grand-Master*'s Chair, or Deputed the High Priest to preserve the Royal Art. Their care of the Temple with the many Buildings they raised, and strong Forts, are mentioned in Holy Writ down to *Josiah*, the last good King of *Judah*.

*Solomon*'s Travellers improved the *Gentiles* beyond Expression, thus the *Syrians* adorned their *Damascus* with a lofty Temple and a Royal Palace. Those of Lesser *Asia* became Excellent *Masons*, particularly at *Sardis* in *Lydia*, and along the Sea Coasts, in the Mercantil Cities as at *Ephesus*.

There the Old Temple of *Diana*, built by some *Japhetites* about the Days of *Moses*, being burnt down about 34 Years after *Solomon*'s death, the Kings of Lesser *Asia* Re-founded and Adorn'd it with 127 Columns of the best Marble each 60 Foot High, and 36 of them were of the most noble Sculpture, by the Direction of *Dresiphon* and *Archiphron*, the Disciples of *Solomon*'s Travellers; but it was not finish'd 'till after 220 Years, in the 7th Year of *Hezekiah* King of *Judah*. A. M. 3283.

This Temple was in Length 425 Foot, and in Breadth 220 Foot, with a due proportioned Height, so Magnificent,

nificent, so Admirable a Fabrick, that it became the third, of the seven Wonders of Art, and the charming Mistress of Lesser *Asia*, which *Xerxes* the avow'd Enemy of Image worship, left standing, while he burnt all the other Temples in his way to *Greece*.

But at last it was burnt down by a vile Fellow, only for the Lust of being talked of in after Ages, (whose Name therefore shall not be mentioned here) on the Birth day of *Alexander* the Great, after it had stood 365 Years, about A. M. 3680, when Jocose People said, the Goddess was so deeply engaged at the Birth of her Hero in *Pella* of *Macedonia*, that she had no Leisure to save her Temple at *Ephesus*. It was Re-built by the Architect *Denocrates* at the Expence of the Neighbouring Princes.

The *Assyrians*, ever since *Nimrod* and *Ninus*, had cultivated the Royal art, Especially at their great *Niniveh*, down to King *Pul* (to whom *Jonas* Preached) and his Son *Sardan Pul* or *Sardanapulus*, called also *Tonos Consoleus*, who was Besieged by his Brother *Tiglath Pul Eser* and his General *Nabonasar*, 'till he burnt himself with his Concubines and Treasure in Old *Nimrod's* Palace, in the 12th Year of *Jotham* King of *Judah*, * A. M. 3257, when the Empire was Partitioned between *Tiglath Pul Eser*, who succeeded at *Niniveh*, and *Nabonassar* who got *Chaldea*.

*Nabonassar*

---

* *Assyria*, A. M 3257. *Sardanapalus* being Dead,

1st. *Tiglath-Pul Eser*, called also *Arbaces* and *Ninus* Junr. succeeded at *Niniveh* and Died A. M. 3275.

2d. *Salman-Eser* Died 3289.

3d. His Son *Senacherib* Died 3297.

4th. *Eser Haddon* succeeded his Father *Senacherib*, and after he had Reigned at *Niniveh* 27 Years he took in *Babylon* at the End of the Interregnum An. Nabon. 67. A. M. 3324 and so annex'd *Chaldæa* again to *Assyria*, he Died 3336.

5th *Soas-*

*Nalonaffar*, called also *Belefis* or *Baladan*, an Excellent Astronomer and Architect, built his new Metropolis upon the ruins of a part of Old *Nimrod*'s Works near the great Tower of Old *Babel* then standing, and

---

5th *Saofduchinus* call'd in *Judith*, *Nabucodonofor* Died 3365.
6th. *Chiniladanus* Slain by his General *Nabopolaffer*, 3378.
7th. *Saracus* Slain by *Nabopolaffar* 3392 *Nabopolaffar* sometimes call'd *Nebuchadnezzar* the 1st Then seiz'd *Chaldæa* and Reigned on the Throne of Old *Nabonaffar* at *Babylon* 14 Years, 'till he destroy'd *Saracus* A. M 3392.

1st. *Nabopolaffar* willing to please his Allies the *Medes*, demolish'd the Great *Niniveh*. Thus *Babylon* was now the Capital of the *Affyrian* Empire. He died 3399.

2d. *Nebuchadnezzar*, who captivated the Jews and adorn'd *Babylon*, died 3442.

3d *Evil Merodach* Slain A M 3444
4th. N. N Wife of *Neriglisar*, who flew *Evil Merodach* and Reigned 3 Years.

5th. *Laborofoarchod* Reigned 1 Year.
6th *Belshazzar* succeeded *Laborofoarchod* and was slain by *Cyrus*, A. M. 3465.

* *Media*. The *Medes* revolting from *Senacherib* King of *Affyria* A. M 3296, chuse for their King,

1st. *Dejoces* who enlarg'd and adorn'd his Capital *Ecbatana* 'till slain in Battle by the *Affyrians* 3348.

2d. *Pharaortes*, died 3370
3d. *Cyaxares* the 1st. was the Patron of the Learned in the East and died 3410.

4th. *Astyages*, Married *Ariena* Sister of *Crœsus* King of *Lydia*. He died 3445, leaving a Son and two Daughters, *viz*. *Mandane* the Eldest, *Amytas* the other.

*Mandane* the eldest Daughter, Wife of *Cambyses* a *Persian* Prince call'd by some King of *Persia*, Father and Mother of *Cyrus* the Great; who began the *Persian* Monarchy 3468.

*Amytis* was the other Daughter of *Astyages* King of *Media*.

*Cyaxares* the 2d. King of *Media*, call'd in Scripture *Darius* the *Mede*. He join'd his Nephew and Son-in-law *Cyrus* in his Wars; Reign'd at *Babylon* after *Belshazzar* two Years, died 3467.

*Caffendana* was the Heiress of *Media* and wife of *Cyrus*, She was Daughter to *Cyaxares* the 2d.

*Cambyses* King of *Perfia*. See Chap IV.

call'd

call'd it *Babylon*, founded in the first Year of the *Nabonaſſarin* Æra A. M. 3257.

For this City *Babylon*, is not mentioned in any Author * before *Iſaiah*, who mentions both its rise and ruin. Chap. xxiii. 13.

*Nabonaſſar* Reign'd 14 Years, ſucceeded by four Kings who Reign'd twelve Years, 'till his Son was of Age, viz *Merodach Baladan*, or *Mardoch Empadus*, who Reign'd twelve Years, and after him five more Kings, tho' not of his Iſſue, who Reign'd twenty one Years. Then follow'd an Interregnum of eight Years, ending An. Nabon 67.

The Science and the Art long flouriſh'd in Eaſtern *Aſia*, to the fartheſt *Eaſt-Indies*. But alſo before the Days of *Nebuchadnezzar* the Great, we find that Old *Maſonry* took a Weſtern courſe; for the Diſciples of *Solomon's* Travellers, by the Encouragement of Princes and States Weſt of the *Aſſyrian* bounds, Built, Enlarged and Adorn'd Cities paſt number, as appears from the Hiſtory of their Foundations in many Books of Chronology §.

After Godly *Joſiah* King of *Judah* fighting for his Superior, *Nabopolaſſer*, was ſlain in the battle of *Hadad Rimmon* by *Pharoah Necho*, *

* A. M. 3394 all things went wrong in *Judah*. For
B. C. 610 the Grand Monarch *Nebuchadnezzar*, firſt his Father's Partner having defeated *Necho*, made *Joſiah's* Son *Jehoiakim* his Vaſſal,

---

* See *Marſham's* Cannon. Sect. 17.

§ Such as *Boriſthenes* and *Sinope* in *Pontus*: *Nicomedia*, *Pruſias* and *Chalcedon* in *Bithynia*: *Bizantium* (now *Conſtantinople*) *Cyzicus* alſo and *Lampſacus* in the *Heleſpont*: *Abdera* in *Thrace*: many Cities in Greece: *Tarentum*, *Regium*, *Rome*, *Ravenna*, *Crotona*, *Florence*, and many more in *Italy*: *Granada*, *Malaga*, *Gades*, &c. in *Spain*: *Maſſilia* and others on the Coaſt of Gaul: while *Britain* was unknown.

and

and for his revolting he ruin'd him, and at Length Captivated all the remaining Royal Family of *Judah* with the flower of the Nobles, especially of the more Ingenious *Crafts-men*, laid waste the whole Land of *Israel*, burnt and demolished all the fine Edifices, and also the Glorious and Inimitable Temple of *Solomon*, after it was finish'd and ⎱ A. M 3416 ⎰ oh lamentable! Consecrated 416 Years, ⎰ B. C. 588 ⎱

Mean while *Nebuchadnezzer* was carrying on his Grand Design of Inlarging and Beautifying *Babylon*, and employ'd the more skillful Artists of *Judah*, and his other captivated Nations to join the *Chaldees* in raising the Walls, the Palaces, the Hanging Gardens, the amazing Bridge, the Temples, the long and broad Streets, the Squares, &c, of that proud Metropolis, accounted the fourth, of the seven Wonders of Art, described at large in many Books, therefore needless to be Rehearsed Particularly here.

But for all his unspeakable Advantages of Wealth and Power, and for all his vast Ambition, he could not arrive at the sublime of the Solomonian Stile. 'Tis true, after his Wars, he was a mighty Encourager of Architecture, a sumptuous *Grand-Master*; and his Artists discover'd great Knowledge in raising his Golden Image in the Vale of *Dura* sixty Cubits high and six broad, and also in all the beautiful parts of his great *Babylon*: Yet it was never fully Peopled; for his Pride provok'd God to afflict him with brutal Madness for 7 Years, and when restored, he lived about one year only and died.\* But    A. M. 3442 23 Years after, his Grandson *Belshazzar* was slain by *Cyrus*, who conquered that Empire and soon removed the Throne to *Susiana* in *Persia*.

The *Medes* and *Persians* had much improved in the Royal Art, and had rivall'd the *Assyrians* and *Chaldeans* in *Masonry* at *Ekbeatana*, *Susiana*, *Persepolis*, and many more fine Cities, before they conquer'd them in War; tho' they had nothing so large as *Niniveh* and *Babylon*, nor so accurate as the Temple, and the other Structures of *Solomon*.

    The Jewish Captives, after *Nebuchadnezzar*'s death, kept themselves at Work in regular *Lodges*; 'till the set time of their Deliverance; and were thus the more Capable at the Reduction, of Re-building the Holy Temple and City of *Salem* upon the old Foundations; which was order'd by the Decree of *Cyrus*, according to Gods word, that had foretold his Exaltation and that Decree publish'd *.

\* A. M. 3468
  B. C.  536

C H A P.

# CHAP. IV.

## From *Cyrus* to *Grand-Master* SELEUCUS NICATOR.

1. CYRUS now King of Kings, having founded the *Persian* Monarchy * made his famous Decree to Re-build the Temple of *Jerusalem* and Constituted, for his Provincial *Grand-Master* in *Judah*, *Zerubbabel* the Lineal Heir of *David*'s Royal Race, and Prince of the Reduction, with the High Priest *Jeshua* his Deputy; who next Year founded the second Temple. *Cyrus* built a great Palace near *Saras* in *Persia*, but before *Zerubbabel* had half finished, the good *Cyrus* died §.

* A. M. 3468
B. C. 536

§ A. M. 3474

2. *Cambyses* neglected the Temple, being wholly intent upon the Conquest of *Egypt*, that had revolted under *Amasis*, the last of *Mitzraims* Race, a learned *Grand-Master*; for whom the *Fellow-crafts* cut out of a Rock, an House all of one Stone 21 Cubits long, 12 broad, and 8 deep, the Labour of 2000 *Masons* for 3 Years, and brought it safe to *Memphis*.

He built many costly Structures, and contributed largely to the Rebuilding of Appollo's Temple at *Delphi* in *Greece*, and died † much lamented just as *Cambyses* had reached to *Egypt*.

† A. M. 3478

*Cambyses* conquer'd the land, and destroy'd many Temples, Palaces, Obelisks, and other glorious Monuments of the Antient *Egyptian Masonry*, and died ‖ on his way home.

‖ A. M. 3482

E 2

3. The

3. The false *Smerdis*, the *Magian*, usurped part of this Year, call'd by *Ezrah Artaxerxes*, who stopt the building of the Temple.

4. *Darius Hystaspes*, one of the 7 Princes that cut off *Smerdis*, succeeded, married *Artistona* the Daughter of *Cyrus*, and confirm'd his Decree.

So that in the 6th Year, just 20 Years after the founding of the Temple, *Zerubbabel* finished it * and Celebrated the Cape-
\* A. M. 3489
B. C. 515 stone; and next Year its Consecration or Dedication was Solemniz'd.

And tho' it came far short of *Solomon*'s Temple in Extent and Decorations; nor had in it the Cloud of Glory or Divine *Shechinah*, and the Holy Religion of *Moses*, yet, being rear'd in the Solomonian stile, it was the finest Building on Earth.

In this reign *Zoroastres* flourish'd, the *Archimagus* or *Grand-Master* of the *Magians* (who worshiped the Sun and Fire made by its Rays) who became famous every where, call'd by the *Greeks*, the Teacher of all Human and Divine Knowledge; and his Disciples were great Improvers of Geometry and the Liberal Arts, ejecting many Palaces and *Fire Temples* throughout the Empire, and long flourish'd, in Eastern *Asia*, even 'till the *Mahometans* prevail'd, yet a Remnant of them are scatter'd in those parts to this Day, who retain many of the Old Usages of the *Free-Masons*, for which they are here mention'd, and not for their Religious Rites that are not the Subject of this Book: For we leave every Brother to Liberty of Conscience; but strictly charge him carefully to maintain the Cement of the *Lodge*, and the three Articles of *Noah*.

*Zoroastres* was slain by *Argasp* the *Scythian*, A. M. 3517, and *Hystaspes* died, 3518.

5 *Xerxes* his Son, succeeded, who encouraged the *Magian Masons*, and destroy'd all the Image Temples
(except

(except that of *Diana* at *Ephesus*) in his way to Greece, with an Army of 5 Millions, and Ships past number: But the Confederate Greeks shamefully beat this common Enemy both at Sea and Land, A. M. 3525, at last *Xerxes* was Murder'd, A. M. 3529.

6. *Artaxerxas Longimanus* his Son succeeded, call'd *Ahashuerus*; and he Married the handsome Jewish Queen *Hester*, in his third Year he made a Feast during 6 Months, for all his Princes and Servants, at his Palace of *Susan* or *Susiana*; and the Drinking was according to the Law; none was compell'd, for so the King had appointed to all the Officers of his House, that they should do according to every Man's pleasure, Est. 1. 5. &c.

He sent *Ezra* the learned Scribe to succeed *Zerubbabel*, who built *Synagogues* in every City: And next *Nehemiah* who rebuilt the Walls of *Jerusalem*, and obliged the Richer People to fill that City with fine Houses; whereby it recovered its antient Splendor, when *Ahashuerus* died, A. M. 3580.

7. *Xerxes* his Son by Queen *Hester* succeeded, but Reign'd only forty five Days, being Murder'd by

8. *Sogdianus* the Bastard of *Ahashuerus*, who Reign'd six Months 'till destroy'd by

9. *Darius Nothus* another Bastard of that King who Reigned 19 Years.

In his 15 Year *Nehemiah* made his last Reformation; and *Malachi* being dead * we read no more of the Prophets.     * A. M. 3559     B. C. 409

This Year *Nothus*, gave leave to *Sanballat* to build the *Samaritan* Temple on Mount *Gerizzim*, like that of *Jerusalem*, and made his Son in-Law *Manasseh* the High Priest of it; and it stood splendid 'till *John Hircanus*,

*Hircanus*, the *Asmonæan* King and High Priest demolished it: When also he made the Idumeans or Edomites conform to the Law of *Moses*.

{ From the said A. M. 3595
during Years ——— 279
Till A. M. ——— 3874
B. C. ——— 130 }

After *Nehemiah*, the High Priest of *Jerusalem* for the Time being, was the provincial *Grand-Master* of *Judea*, first under the Kings of *Persia*, and afterwards under the *Grecian* Kings of *Egypt* and *Syria*, *Darius Nothus* died A. M. 3599.

10. *Artaxerxes Mnemon* his Son Succeeded 46 Years. He was a great Encourager of the *Craft*, especially after the Ascent of his Brother *Cyrus*, and the Retreat of *Zenophon* A. M. 3603.

In his 12th. Year the brave *Conon* rebuilt the Walls of *Athens*, The King died, A. M. 3645.

11. *Darius Ochus* his Son Succeeded 21 Years. In his 6th. Year A. M. 3651. *Mausolus* King of *Caria*, in Lesser *Asia* died, and next Year his Mournful widow *Artemisia* (also his Sister) founded for him a most Splendid Sepulchral Monument at *Halicarnasus* of the best Marble, (Hence all great Tombs are call'd Mausoleum's,) in length from North to South 63 Cubits, in Circuit, 411 foot, and in height 140 foot, Surrounded with 136 Columns of most Accurate Sculpture, and the Fronts East and West had Arches 73 foot wide, with a pyramid on the side Wall, ending in a pointed Broach, on which was a Coach with 4 Horses of one Marble Stone. All was perform'd by the 4 best *Mason* of the age, Viz. *Scopas*, *Leochares*, *Timotheus* and *Briax*, it is reckon'd the 5th, of the 7 Wonders of Art.

*Ochus* was Murder'd by his favourite *Eunuch Bagos* who set up,

12. *Arses*

12. *Arses* his youngest Son, (the rest being Murder'd) 3667. But *Bagos* fearing *Arses*, Murder'd him in 2 Years, and set up one of the Royal Family, viz.

13. *Darius Codomannus*, who began to Reign 3669. *Bagos* prepared a Dose of poison for him, but *Darius* made him drink it himself. He Reigned 6 Years, till Conquer'd by *Alexander* the Great.

At length the Royal Art flourish'd in *Greece*. Indeed we read of the Old *Dedalus* and his Sons, the imitators of the *Egyptians* and *Phænicians*, of the little *Labyrinth* in *Crete*, and the Larger at *Lemnos*, of the Arts and Sciences Early at *Athens* and *Sicyon*, *Candia* and *Sicily* before the *Trojan* war; of the Temples of *Jupiter Olympius*, *Esculapius*, &c. of the *Trojan* horse, and other things: But we are all in Darkness, Fable and Uncertainty till the Olympiads.

Now the 35th Year of *Uzziah* King of *Judah* is the first Year of the first Olympiad when some of their bright Men be-⎧ A. M. 3228 ⎫ before the Founding gan to Travel ⎨ B. C. 776 ⎬ *Rome* 28 Years.

So that their most famous Buildings, as the Citadel of *Athenes*, the Court of *Areopagus*, the *Parthenian* or Temple of *Minerva*, the Temples of *Theseus* and *Apollo*, their Porticoes and Forum's, Theatres and Gymnasiums, Stately publick Halls, Curious Bridges, Regular Fortifications, Stout Ships of war, and Magnificent Palaces, with their best Statues and Sculpture, were all of 'em, either at first erected, or else Rebuilt fine, even after the Temple of *Zerubbabel*; for

*Thales Milesius*, their first Philosopher, died Eleven Years only before the Decree of *Cyrus*; and the same Year 3457. *Pythagoras*, his Scholar, Travell'd in *Egypt*; while *Pisistratus*, the Tyrant of *Athens*, began to Collect the first Library in *Greece*.

*Pythagoras* Liv'd 22 Years among the *Egyptian* Priests till sent by *Cambyses* to *Babylon* and *Persia*, A. M. 3480. where he pick'd up great Knowledge among
the

( 40 )

the *Chaldæan Magians* and *Babylonish Jews*; and Return'd to *Greece* the Year that *Zerubbabel*'s Temple was Finish'd A. M. 3489.

He became not only the Head of a new Religion of Patch work, but likewise of an Academy or *Lodge* of good Geometricians, to whom he communicated a Secret viz. * that Amazing proposition which is the foundation of all *Masonry*, of whatever Meterials or Dimensions, call'd by *Masons* his *Heureka*; because they think it was his own Invention.

\* Euclid. lib. 1. Prop. xlvii.

But after *Pythagoras*, Geometry was the Darling study of the *Greeks*, and their learned Men reduced the noble Science to the Use of the Ingenious Mechanicks of all sorts, that perform by Geometry as well as the Operators in Stone or Brick.

And as *Masonry* kept pace with Geometry, So many *Lodges* Appear'd especially in the Grecian Republicks, where Liberty, Trade and Learning flourish'd; as at *Sicyon*, *Athens*, *Corinth* and the Cities of *Jonia*, 'till they arriv'd at their beautiful *Dorick*, *Jonic*, and *Corinthian* orders: And their Improvements were soon discover'd to the *Persians* with a Vengeance, when they defeated *Xerxes*, A. M. 3525.

*Greece* now abounded with the best Architects, Sculptors, Statuaries, Painters and other fine Designers, most of them Educated at the Academies of *Athens* and *Sicyon*, who instructed many Artists, and *Fellow-Crafts*, to be the best Operators upon Earth: So that the Nations of *Asia* and *Africa*, who had taught the Greeks, were now taught by them.

The learned Greeks rightly Judging, that the rules of the beautiful Proportions in Architecture should be taken from the Proportions of the Human Body, their fine Painters and Statuaries were esteem'd Architects, and were then actually so (even as afterwards

true

( 41 )

true old *Masonry* was reviv'd in *I-*
*taly* by the Painters *) nor could they    * See Chap. vii.
have been fine Painters without be-
ing Architects.

Therefore several of those Excellent Painters and
Philosophers, § are in the List of Antient Architects:
Nay they all openly taught Geometry, and many of
them practis'd *Masonry*; and being Gentlemen of good
repute, they were generally at the Head of the *Craft*,
highly useful to the *Fellow Crafts*, by their Designs
and fine Drawings, and bred them up clever Artists:
Only by a Law in *Greece*, no Slave was allow'd to learn
the seven Liberal Sciences, or those of the Free-born †;
so that in *Greece* also they were called *Free-Masons*, and
in their many *Lodges*, the noble and Learned were accepted as Brothers, down to the Days of *Alexander* the
Great, and afterwards for many Ages.

That Warlike Prince, began to
Reign in *Macedonia* * a little before    * A. M. 3669.
*Darius Codomannus* began in *Persia*,    B. C. 335.
and next Year *Alexander* entering *A-*
*sia*, won the Battle of *Granicus*; and next Year the
Battle of *Issus*, and next Year took in *Tyre* and *Gaza*,
and over-ran *Egypt*; and next Year won the Battle of

---

§ No Country but Greece could now boast of such Men as
Micon, Phidias, Demon, Androcides, Meton, Anaxagoras,
Dipœnus and Scyllis, Glycon, Alcamenes, Praxitiles, Polycle-
tus, Lysippus, Peneus, Euphranor, Perseus, Philistratus,
Zeuxis, Appollodorus, Parhasius, Timanthes, Eupompus,
Pamphilus, Apelles, Artemones, Socrates, Eudoxu, Metrodo-
rus, (who wrote of Masonry, and the excellent Theodorus Cy-
renæus who amplify'd Geometry, and publish'd the
Art Analytic, then Master of the Di-    * Plato died A M. 3656.
vine Plato*, from whose School came
Xenocrates and Aristotle the Preceptor of Alexander the Great.

† According to the Old Constitutions these are, 1. Grammer,
2. Rhetoric. 3d. Logic. 4 Arithmetic, 5, Geometry. 6.
Music. 7. Astronomy.

*Arbela*

*Arbela*, after which poor *Darius*, flying into *Bactria*, was Murder'd by his General *Bessus*, after he had Reign'd 6 Years, after *Cyrus* began 207 Years. { A. M. 3674 / B. C. 330 } When the *Persian* Monarchy Ended and the *Grecian* Commenced.

But tho' from Ambition *Alexander* order'd *Denocrates* the Architect to found *Alexandria* in *Egypt*, yet he is not reckon'd a *Mason*, because at the Instigation of a *Drunken-Whore*, in his Revels, he Burnt the Rich and splendid *Persepolis*, a City of Palaces in the best Stile, which no true *Mason* wou'd do, was he ever so Drunk.

He found the loss of that fine City when he return'd from *India*, but did not retrieve it: Nor did he Encourage the noble Proposal of *Denocrates* to dispose Mount *Athos* in the form of the Kings Statue, with a City in one Hand, and in the other Hand a large Lake to Water the City: Only he destroy'd no more Monuments of Art. Indeed he lov'd *Apelles* who drew his Picture, and *Lysippus* who form'd his Statue, and intended to Encourage Arts and Sciences throughout the World;

\* A. M. 3680
B. C. 324

but he was prevented by dying Drunk at *Babylon*, 6 Years after *Codomannus*\*.

*Alexander* left his New Grecian Monarchy to be partition'd among his Generals, which may be said to commence 12 Years after his Death,

§ A. M. 3692
B. C. 312

when *Seleucus Nicator* took in *Babylon*, and began the *Seleucian* Æra §.

CHAP.

# CHAP. V.

## From *Seleucus*, to *Grand-Master* AUGUSTUS CÆSAR.

SELEUCUS NICATOR prov'd an Excellent *Grand-Master*, founded the great *Seleucia* on the Euphrates for his *Deputy* in the *East*; and in the *West*, he built his stately Capital City, the famous *Antioch* in old *Syria*, with the great Grove of *Daphne*; a sacred *Asylum*, in the middle of which he rear'd the Temple of *Apollo* and *Diana* (tho' it prov'd afterwards the Temple of *Venus* and *Bacchus*) and also the lesser Cities of Old *Syria*, as *Apamia*, *Berræa*, *Seleucia*, *Laodicea*, *Edessa*, *Pella*, &c. and having Reigned thirty three Years he died, A. M. 3725.

*Antiochus Soter* succeeded his Father and died A. M. 3744.

*Antiochus Treos* succeeded his Father and died A. M. 3759 the Progenitor of a long Royal race that were all set aside by *Pompey*.

But in the 4th Year of *Theos*,

*Arsaces*, a noble *Parthian*, revolted from the SyroGrecian Kings, and founded the famous Kingdom of *Parthia*, Anno Eræ Seleuci 57. * in Eastern *Asia*, that in time set bounds to the Romans.   \* A. M. 3748  B. C. 256

Yet the *Arsacidæ*, and also the *Seleucidæ*, being chiefly conversant in War, we must travel into *Egypt*, to find the best *Free-Masons*, where the Grecian Architecture flourish'd under *Ptolemaidæ*. For

*Ptolemy*

( 44 )

*B. M. 3700
A. C. 304

*Ptolemy Soter*, had set up his Throne at *Alexandria*, which he much inlarged and beautifi'd*.

*Euclid* the *Tyrian* came to *Ptolemy* in this first Year, who had collected in his Travels the scatter'd Elements of Geometry, and Digested them into a Method that was never yet mended; for which his Memory will be Fragrant in the Lodges to the end of Time.

*Ptolemy*, Grand-Master, † with *Euclid* the Geometrician and *Straton* the Philosopher, as *Grand-Wardens*, built his Palace at *Alexandria*, and the curious *Musæum* or *Colledge* of the Learned, with the Library of *Brucheum* near the Palace, that was filled with 400,000 Books, or valuable Manuscripts, before it was burnt in the Wars of *Julius Cæsar*.

*Soter* Died——            —— A. M. 3719

*Ptolemy Philadelphus*, succeeded his Father in the Throne and *Solomon*'s Chair too: And in his second Year he carried on the great Tower of *Pharo*, founded by his Father, § the 6th of the seven Wonders of Art, built on an Island, as the light House for the Harbour of *Alexandria*, (whence light Houses in the Mediterranean are call'd *Faros*) a piece of amazing Architecture, by the care of the *Grand-Wardens*, *Dexiphanes* and his Son *Sostratus*, the Father built the Heptasta-

---

† According to the Traditions, and the Old Constitutions.

§ Some prefer to this, the great Obelisk of Queen *Semiramis* 150 Foot high and 24 Foot square at Bottom, all of one intire Stone like a Pyramid, that was brought from *Armenia* to *Babylon*, Also an Huge Rock cut into the Figure of *Semiramis*, with the smaller Rocks by it in the shape of Tributary Kings: If we may believe *Ctesias* against the advice of *Berosus* and *Aristotle*: For she is not so antient as is generally thought, and seems to be only the Queen of *Nabonassar*.

dium

dium for joining the Island to the Continent, while the Son Rear'd the Tower.

*Philadelphus* founded the City of *Ajyos Hormus* on the Red Sea for the *East India Trade*, built the Temple of the *Zephyrian Venus* in *Crete*, *Ptolemais* in *Palestine*, and rebuilt Old *Rabbah* of the *Ammonites*, calling it *Philadelphia*. Nay he was so accurate an Architect, that for a long time all fine Masonry was call'd *Philadelphian*, or after the Stile of *Philadelphus*, he died A. M. 3757.

*Ptolemy Euergetes* his Son, succeeded the great Encourager of the *Craft*, with his two *Grand Wardens*, his learned Librarians, viz. *Eratosthenes* of *Cyrene*, and *Apollonius* of *Perga*. the Library of *Brucheum* being near full, he erected that of *Serapium*, which in time contain'd 300,000 Manuscripts, to which *Cleopatra* added 200,000 more from the Library of *Pergamus* given to her by *Mark Anthony*; but all were burnt in Ovens by the Ignorant *Saracens* to bake Bread for their Army*, to the last-    * A. D. 642 ing and Irreparable Damage of the Learned.

*Euergetes* was the last good *Grand Master* of *Egypt*; and therefore we shall sail over to the *Hellespont* to view the glorious Temple of *Cyzicus*, with threads of beaten Gold in the Joynts of the insides of the Marble-stones, that cast a fine Lustre on all the Statues and Images; besides the curious Eccho of the 7 Towers at the *Thracian* Gate of *Cyzicus*, and a large *Bouleuterian* or *Town House*, without one Pin or Nail in the Carpenters Work; so that the Beams and Rafters could be taken off, and again put on, without Laces or Keys to bind them.

The *Rhodians* also employ'd *Cares* (the Scholar of *Lysippus*) the Architect, to erect the great *Colossus* of *Rhodes*, the last of the seven Wonders of Art, made of Metal, the greatest human Statue under the Sun, to whom it was Dedicated.

It was 70 Cubits high, and duly Proportioned in every Part and Limb, ſtriding in the Harbour's Mouth, wide enough to receive between his Legs the largeſt Ship under Sail, and appearing at a Diſtance like an High Tower

It began in the 4th Year of *Pto-lemy Soter* ——————— A. M. 3704
And Finiſh'd in Years  ——————  12
—————
3716
It ſtood firm Years ———————  66
—————
And fell by an Earthquake ————— 3782
B. C. ——— 222

The laſt Year of *Ptolomey Euergetes*.
The great *Colloſſus* lay in Ruins, Years —— 894
Even till A. D ———————— 672
When *Mahowias* the 6th Caliph of the *Saracens* carried it off to *Egypt*, the Load of 900 *Camels*.

Tho' ſome prefer to it the Statue of *Jupiter Olympius* ſitting on a fine Throne in his Old Dorick Temple of *Achaia*, made of Innumerable pieces of Porphyre, Gold and Ivory, exceeding grand, and exactly proportioned: For tho' the Temple was in Height 68 Foot clear, *Jupiter* could not ſtand upright. It was perform'd by the great *Phidias*, as was that of *Nemeſis* at *Rhamnus*, 10 Cubits high, and that of *Minerva* at *Athens* 26 Cubits high.

While the Greeks were propogating the Science and the Art in the very beſt manner, founding new Cities, repairing old ones, and erecting Statues paſt Number, the other *Africans* imitated the *Egyptians*, Southward in *Ethiopia* down to the *Cape* of good *Hope*; and alſo Weſtward to the *Atlantic* Shore: Tho' Hiſtory fails, and no Travellers have yet diſcover'd the valuable remains of thoſe many powerful Nations.

Only

Only we know that the *Carthaginians* had form'd a Magnificent Republic long before the Romans; had built some thousands of stately Cities and strong Castles, and made their great Capital *Carthage* the Terror of *Rome*, and her rival for Universal Empire. Great was their skill in Geometry and Masonry of all sorts, in Marble Temples, Golden Statues, Stately Palaces, Regular Forts, and Stout Ships that Sail'd in all the known Seas, and carried on the chief Trade of the known World: Therefore the Emulous Romans long designed its Destruction, having a Prophetical Proverb, *Delenda est Cathago! Carthage* must be Demolish'd; which they accomplish'd as in the Sequel.

Thus *Hannibal* the Warlike, in his retreat from *Carthage* to *Armenia*, shew'd his great skill in Drawing for King *Artaxes* the plan of the City *Artaxata*, and Survey'd the Palace, Temples and Citadel thereof.

The Learned *Sicilians*, descended from the Greeks, follow'd their Instructions in Architecture throughout the Island very early, at *Agrigentum, Messana, Gela*, &c. Especially at *Syracuse*; for when it was Besieged by the Romans it was 22 Miles round, and *Marcellus* could not Storm it, because of the amazing devices of the Learned Geometrician, Architect, Mechanic and Engineer, the Noble *Archimedes* * till by Mastering an ill-guarded Tower, the City was taken by surprize on a Festival Day. But tho' *Marcellus* gave a strick charge to save *Archimedes*, a common Soldier slew him, while, not minding the uproar, the Noble and Learned Man was deeply engaged in Mechanical Speculations and Schemes to repulse the Romans and save *Syracuse*.

---

* Call'd by the Old *Masons* the Noble and Excellent *Grand Master* of *Syracuse*.

*Marcellus*

*Marcellus* shed Tears for him as a Public loss to the Learned, and gave him an Honourable Burial,

| | |
|---|---|
| A. M. | 3792 |
| In the Year of Rome | 537 |
| B. C. | 212 |

While *Hannibal* Distress'd *Italy*.

Many of the Grecian, *Carthaginian*, and *Sicilian Masons* had Travell'd into the *North* and *West* of *Europe*, and propogated their useful skill, Particularly in *Italy*, *Spain*, the *Balearic Islands*, and the Coasts of *Gaul*, but History fails, 'till the Roman Armies came there. Nor have we certain Accounts of the *Chinese* and other *East Indians*, 'till the Europeans Navigated Thither in these latter Times; only the Wall of *China* makes a Figure in the Map, tho' we know not yet when it was Built: Also their great Cities and Splendid Palaces, as describ'd by Travellers, Evidently discover that those Antient Nations had long cultivated Arts and Sciences, especially Geometry and Masonry.

Thus hitherto the *Masons*, above all other Artists, have been the favourites of the Eminent, who wisely Joyn'd the Lodges for the better Conducting of their various Undertakings in old Architecture: And still great Men Continued at the Head of the *Craft*; as will appear in the Sequel.

From *Sicily* we soon pass into *Italy*, to view the first Improvements of the Romans, who for many Ages affected nothing but War, 'till by degrees they learned the Science and the Art from their Neighbours. But,

The *Hetrurians* or *Tuscans* very early used their own natural *Tuscan* Order, never used by the Greeks, and were the first in *Italy* that learned the Greeks the *Doric*, *Ionic*, and *Corinthian* Orders; 'till the Royal Art was there Conspicuous under their King *Porsenna*, who built a stately Labyrinth, not Inferior to that of *Lemnos*, and the Highest Mausoleum on Record.

*Porsenna*

( 49 )

*Porsenna* died in the Year of Rome    303,
A. M. ——————— ——————— 3558
B. C. ——————— ——————— 446

the 19th Year of *Artaxerxes Longimanus*, while the Romans were only engaged in Subduing their Neighbours in *Italy*, and their Taste was yet but low; 'till

*Turrenus*, the last King of the *Tuscans*, bequeathed his Kingdom to the Romans; in the 6th Year of *Philadelphus*, while *Pyrrhus* distress'd *Italy*. *Turrenus* died, A. M. 3724. The *Tuscans* had built many fine strong Places, and now their Disciples were invited to *Rome*, and taught the Romans the Royal Art, tho' still their Improvements were not considerable, 'till

*Marcellus*, Triumphed in the splendid spoils of *Syracuse*, upon the Death of the great *Archimedes* as above.

*Marcellus* the Patron of Arts and Sciences, employ'd his *Fellow Crafts* to build at *Rome* his famous Theatre, with a Temple to Virtue, and another to Honour; yet the High Taste of the Romans was not General, 'till *Scipio Asiaticus* led them against *Antiochus Magnus* King of *Syria*, and took from him all the Country West of Mount *Taurus* in the 15th Year of *Ptolemy Epiphanes* { A. M. 3814 } In the Year { B. C. 190 } of *Rome* 559 for then, with Astonishment, they beheld the unspeakable Beauties of the *Grecian* and *Asiatic* Architecture, standing in full Splendor, which they resolv'd to Imitate. And so they went on Improving, 'till

*Scipio Africanus* (who had always a set of the Learned attending him as their Patron) took in the Great Rival of *Rome* the Glorious *Carthage*, which he Demolish'd against his own Inclination by Command of the Senate; for *Delenda est Carthago* the Account of its Destruction is Lamentable. { A. M. 3858 } Year of *Rome* { B. C. 146 } 603

while Consul *Mummius* the same Year sack'd *Corinth*,

G            the

( 50 )

the wealthy Queen of Greece, who Discover'd his Ignorance, when he threatned those that carried home, from *Corinth*, the Inimitable Pictures of *Hercules* and *Bacchus*, that if they lost them, they must make them good with new ones.

Both these Generals Triumphed at *Rome* in the portable Monuments of Art, brought from those Cities, that had been the most Opulent and Glorious upon Earth. But now the *Romans* were so wise as to bring home too the ablest professors of Science, and Practitioners of Art. After which we read of several stately Edifices at *Rome*, built in the finest Grecian Stile; as the famous Palace of *Paulus Emilius* of best *Phrygian* Marble; the Triumphal Arch of *Marius* at *Orange* in *Gaul*, the three Surprizing *Theatres* of * *Scaurus* at *Rome*, &c.

The mighty *Sylla* brought the Columns of the Temple of *Jupiter Olympius* from *Greece*, to adorn the Temple of *Jupiter Capitolinus* at *Rome*, after the old one, built by *Tarquinius Superbus*, was Burnt; in whose time *Jupiter* was only of Clay, but now of pure Gold.

*Lucullus*, the Learned and Brave, Erected a fine Library, and a Splendid House with Gardens, in the Asiatic Stile.

*Pompey* the Great, built a Theatre that held 40,000 People at the shows, near his fine Palace and Temple of Victory.

---

* The one held 80000 People at the Shows or Plays. It had 3 Scenes or Lofts one above another, with 360 Columns: The first row of Marble, each 38 Foot High, the second row was of Christial, and the 3d of Gilded Wood: Between the Columns were 3000 Statues of Brass.

The other two Theatres were of Wood, Sustained on great Axles, whereby they could be turned round, and join'd in one Amphi-Theatre. Plin.

These

These and other great Men, During the Roman Republick, much encouraged Architects and *Masons* as their Patrons; and in their Absence, the Consul Resident, or the High Priest of *Rome*, or the Arch Flamin, or some other great Man on the spot, thought it his Honour to be the Patron of Arts and Sciences (what we now call *Grand Masters*) attended duly by the most Ingenious of the Fraternity; 'till the Republic was near its Exit by the Competition of *Pompey* and *Cæsar* for Pre-eminence.

But *Pompey* being routed at *Pharsalia*, and Murdered by the *Egyptians* in his flight, the Republic expir'd, and *Julius Cæsar* obtained the Pre-eminence.

|  |  |
|---|---|
| A. M. | 3956 |
| Year of *Rome* | 701 |
| B. C. | 48 |
| Before the Birth of Christ | 44 |

*Cæsar* now perpetual Dictator and Imperator, a learned Geometrician, Architect, Engineer and Astronomer, being High Priest, reformed the Roman Kalender, B. C. or before the Christian Æra ——— 45

He and his Legions had built much in *Gaul*, and at *Rome* he Raised his great Circus or Square, a true Oblong, 3 Furlongs in Length, and one in Breadth, that held 260,000 People at the Shows; also his stately Palace, and lovely Temple of *Venus*, and ordered *Carthage* and *Corinth* to be Re-built, about 100 Years after they were Demolished *.

But *Cæsar*, intending first to Quell the *Parthians*; and then, as *Grand Master* of the *Roman* Republic, to Encourage the Science and the Art beyond all before him in Universal Peace, was basely Murdered by his ungrateful *Brutus* under *Pompey*'s Statue; upon which

---

* See *Pliny* who gives a full Account of these things.

A. M. 3960
B. C. 44

the Civil Wars ended, and the Preeminence was in Suspence during 14 Years, 'till *Brutus* and *Cassius* were lost at *Philippy*, and next *Mark Anthony* was Defeated at *Actium* by *Octavianus*, who then Conquer'd *Egypt*, and finish'd the Civil Wars. And so the Grecian Monarchy being fully

A. M. 3974

ended the *Roman* Empire began in the Year of *Rome* 719. Before the Christian Æra 30.

CHAP.

( 53 )

# HAP. V.

## From *Augustus* 'ti the Havock of the GOTHS.

ROME, now the Mistress of the known World, became the Center of Learning as of Imperial Power, and arrived at her Zenith, under

*Octavianus*, now call'd *Sebastor*, or *Augustus Cæsar*, who patroniz'd the Fraternity as their Illustrious *Grand aster*, (so call'd always by Old *Masons*) with his Deputy *Agrippa*, who adorned the *Campus Martius*, and built the grand *Portico* of the *Rotunda Pantheon*, with many more Charming Piles mention'd in History.

*Vitruvius* the Learned, the Principal *Warden*, by his Writings has justly acquir'd the Character of the Father or Teacher of all accurate Architects, and clever Connoisseurs to this Day.

*Augustus* first employ'd his Fellow Crafts in repairing all the Public Edifices (a most needful Work after the Wars) and in rebuilding some of them. But also he built the Bridge of *Ariminum*; and at *Rome* the Temple of *Mars* the *Avenger*, the Temple of *Apollo*, the *Rotunda* call'd *Galucio*, the great and Sumptuous *Forum*, the Principle and Magnificent Palace of *Augustus*, with some Lesser Palaces, the fine *Mausoleum*, the accurate Statue in the Capitol, the curious Library, the Portico, and the Park for the People to walk in, &c. Nay he fill'd the Temples of *Rome* with the most costly Statues, and wittily set up that of *Cleopatra* (of Massy Gold brought from *Egypt*) in the Temple of *Venus*.

In those Golden Days of *Augustus*, the Eminent following his Example, built above 100 Marble Palaces at

*Rome*

*Rome*, fit for the greatest Kings; and every Substantial Citizen rebuilt their Houses too in Marble, all joyning in the same Disposition of adorning *Rome*: Whereby many Lodges appear'd, in City and Suburbs, of the *Free and Accepted Masons*: So that *Augustus*, when a Dying, justly said, I found *Rome* built of Brick, but I leave it built of Marbe !

Therefore the present remains of Antient *Rome* in his Time, and of some following Emperors, are so Accurate, that they are the best Patterns of true *Masonry* extant, the Epitome of all the old Grecian Architecture, commonly Expressed by the *Augustan* Stile: And we now wish to arrive at its Glorious Perfection in Wisdom Strength, and Beauty.

But before the Death of *Augustus*, we must Travel into *Judæa*. The High Priests of *Jerusalem* had been Provincial *Grand-Masters* there, nnder the Kings of *Egypt* then Soveraigns of the *Jews*, 'till *Seleucus Philopater* King of *Syria* seiz'd *Judea*, or *Palestine*.\* His Son viz. *Antiochus Epiphanes* cruelly presecuted the Jews, 'till rescued by the Valiant *Asmonæan* Priest *Judas Maccabæus*: For long after *Zerubbabel* and *Jeshua* the High Priest, an Ordinary Priest, call'd *Asmonæus*, appear'd, not of the House of *Jeshua*, but only of the course of *Joarib*, the great Grandfather of *Mattathias*, the brave Priest of *Modin* and Father of *Maccabæus*.

\* A. M. 3824
B. C. 180

For the Lineal Successor of *Jeshua* was *Onias* IV. (Son of *Onias* III. the last good High Priest) who being depriv'd of his right by the *Syrian Kings*, went to *Egypt*, where he got leave to build a Temple at *Heliopolis*, like that at *Jerusalem*, for the *Jews* in *Egypt* and *Cyrene*, then more numerous and Opulent than those in

*Judea*

*Judea.* This Temple was founded,*
A. M. ——————— 3885
B. C. ——————— 149
It stood splendid 'till A. D. 73

During Years ——————— 222
Till Destroy'd *by Vespasion* the Emperor.

But the *Asmonæus* or *Maccabees* fought their way to Pre-eminence against the *Syrian* Kings, and also obtain'd it as High Priests and Princes of the *Jews,* during about 130 Years, 'till *Mark Anthony* and *Octavianus* got the Senate of *Rome* to Create *Herod* the *Edomite,* or *Idumean Jew,* King of *Judea* in the Capitol A. M. 3964, and by the help of the Romans, *Herod* conquer'd *Antigonus,* and mounted the Throne at *Jerusalem.*
A. M. ——————— 3967
Before the Christian Æra ——— 37
Before the Birth of Christ ——— 33

He

---

* *Mattathias* the *Asmonæan* Priest Died A. M. 3837, B. C. 167. and three of his Sons ruled the *Jews,* viz.

1. *Judas Maccabæus,* Died 3843. acted as High Priest and Ruler

2. *Jonathan* owned a Free Prince and High Priest. Murder-ed. 3860.

3. *Simon* the King and High Priest, erected over *Jonathans* Grave a lofty Monument of White Marble

Ruled Independant of the Gentiles, 'till Murder'd A. M. 3868.

4. *John Hyrcanus* succeeded Father *Simon,* 'till he Died, 3897.

5. *Aristobulus* I. Reign'd one Year, viz. A. M. 3898.

6. *Alexander Jannæus* Reign'd 27 Years and Died A. M. 3925 leaving the Crown to,

7. *Alexandra* his Widow, and *Hyrcanus* wore the *Mitre,* 'till she Died, A. M. 3934.

8. *Hyrcanus,* after his Mother Died, was King and High Priest 3 Months, 'till depriv'd by his Brother. He was restored by *Pompey* only to the Mitre, 'till Captivated by the *Parthians,* who set up *Antigonus,* 3964.

*Hyrcannus* was Beheaded by *Herod,* A. M. 3974.

9. *Aristo-*

He got rid of all the *Asmonæans*, made the *Sanhedrim* useless, and set up High Priests at his Pleasure.

But for all his great Faults, *Herod* became the greatest Builder of his Day, the Patron or *Grand Master* of many *Lodges*, and sent the most expert Fellow Crafts of Greece to assist his own *Jews*. For after the Battle of *Actium* B. C. 30. Before Christ's Birth 26.

*Herod*, being reconciled to *Augustus*, began to shew his mighty skill in *Masonry*, by Erecting a splendid Theatre at *Jerusalem*, and next Built the Stately City *Sebaste* (so call'd from *Sebastos* or *Augustus*) formerly *Samaria*, with a curious little Temple in it like that of *Jerusalem*. He made the City *Cæsarea* the best Harbour in *Palestine*, and built a Temple of White Marble at *Paneas*. The Cities *Antipatris*, *Phasaelis* and *Cypron*, and the Tower of *Phasael* at *Jerusalem*, not inferior to the *Pharo* of *Alexandria*, &c.

But his amazing Work was his Re-building of the Temple of *Zerubbabel*, for having prepared materials (which with those of the Old Temple were enough)

---

9. *Aristobulus* II. Usurped Six Years 'till deposed by *Pompey* 3940. And Poisoned, 3955

*Alexandra* Wife of her first Cousin, viz.

*Alexander* Beheaded 3995

10 *Antigonus*, set up by the *Parthians* 3964. Reign'd three Years, 'till conquer'd by *Herod*, and Crucify'd by the *Romans*, 3967.

*Herod* I. an *Idumæan Jew* created at *Rome* King of *Judea* 3964. Conquer'd *Antigonus*, and began to Reign, 3967 And in the last Year of his Reign * ——— 33

*Mariamne*, *Herod*'s Queen, was by him Beheaded, 3975, and by his order her two Sons were Strangled, but they left a Royal Race

*Aristobulus* III. Made High Priest by *Herod*, 'till Drown'd in a Bath without Issue, 3969.

* Christ A. M. 4000, was born, but the first Year of our A. D. or Christian Æra, is A. M. 4004. ee Page 10.

and

and proper Instruments, *Herod* employed 10,000 *Masons* (besides Labourers) and marshall'd them in *Lodges*, under 1000 Priests and Levites that were skillful Architects, as *Masters* and *Wardens* of the *Lodges*, and acted as *Grand-Master* himself, with his Wardens *Hillel* and *Shammai*, two learned Rabbins of great Reputation.

He began to pull down the Temple of *Zerubbabel*, not all at once, but Piece by Piece, and levelled the Foot Stone of this Temple of *Jerusalem*, viz. After the founding of the Second Temple 518 Years; A. M. 3987; in the 21st Year of *Herod*, and 13th Year of *Augustus*, and 29th *Julian* Year, in the 4th Year of *Olympiad*, CXC; and of *Rome* 732, Before the Christian *Æra* 17; before Christ's Birth 14; Just 46 before the second Passover of Christ's Ministry; for the *Jews* said, *Forty-six Years was this Temple in Building.* John xi. 20.

The Holy Place, and the Holy of Holiest in the West, and the great Portico in the East, were finish'd at a wondrous Cost, and in the short Space of one Year and six Months, and the rest, design'd by *Herod*, in eight Years more, nine Years and six Months, when the Fraternity celebrated the Cape-Stone with great Joy, and in due Form; and the King solemnized its Dedication by Prayer and Sacrifice, on his Co-Coronation Day; * of the 31st Year of his Reign, and 23d of *Augustus*.

\* A. M. 3997
B. C. Æ 7
B. C. 3

*Josephus* describes it, † as he view'd it, with Additions built after *Herod* died, a Number of the most curious and magnificent Marble Edifices that had been rais'd since the Days of *Solomon*; yet more after the *Grecian* Stile, and much inferior to *Solomon*'s Tem

---

† Antiq. Lib. xv. Cap. xi.

ple in Extent and Decoration; tho' larger than that of *Zerubbabel*, and was by the *Romans* esteemed the same; for *Tacitus* calls it the same that *Pompey* walk'd thro'. But it was not fully finish'd, in all its Apartments, till about six Years before it was destroy'd, A. D. 64.

At length *Augustus* having shut up the Temple of *Janus*, for that all the World was at Peace, in the 26th Year of his Empire, after the Conquest of *Egypt*, the Word was made Flesh, or the Lord *Jesus Christ Immanuel* was born, the Great Architect, or *Grand-Master* of the Christian Church. After *Solomon*'s Death 971; in the Year of *Rome*, 745; in the Year of *Herod*, 34; in the Year of the *Julian* Period, 4710; in the Year of Masonry, or A. M. 4000; B. C. or before the Christian *Æra*, 4.

King *Herod* died a few Months after the Birth of *Christ*; and, notwithstanding his vast Expence in Masonry, he died rich.

After the Birth of *Christ* four Years, or when *Christ* was going into his fourth Year, the Christian *Æra* begins, A. M. 4004, commonly called, *Anno Domini* 1. See Page 10.

And when *Christ* was aged near 18 Years, the Great *Augustus* died, at *Nola* in *Campania*, *Aug*. 19. A. D. 14; in the Year of *Rome* 761; after he had reigned 44; in the Vulgar Year of *Masonry* 4014; tho' the Accurate Year is 4018 Years; when *Tiberius* I. his Collegue, began to reign alone, who also encouraged the Craft.

In his 20th Year after *Augustus*, or the Vulgar A. D. 34. The Lord *Jesus Christ*, aged 36 Years, and about six Months, was crucified, without the Walls of *Jerusalem*, by *Pontius Pilate* the *Roman* Governor of *Judea*, and rose again from the Dead on the Third Day, for the Justification of all that believe in him.

*Tiberius*

*Tiberius* banish'd *Pontius Pilate* for his Injustice to *Christ*; and next Year that Emperor died. A. D. 35.

The *Augustan* Stile was well cultivated, and the clever Craftsmen were much encouraged by some following Emperors. Thus even

*Nero*, for all his gross Faults, rais'd his brazen Statue in *Via Sacra* 110 Foot high, and built his guilded Palace, a Nonsuch.

*Vespasian*, who commenc'd A. D. 68. sent his brave Son *Titus* to subdue the *Jews*. *Titus* took in *Jerusalem*, when a Soldier, without Orders, set Fire to the Temple *, *Vespasian* shut the Temple of *Janus*, and built the Temple of Peace. He rais'd his    * A. D. 70 A. C. Cru. 36 famous Amphi-theatre, when the rich Composite Order was first used. He order'd the Jewish Temple in *Egypt* to be demolish'd, A. D. 73, and died A, D. 77.

*Titus* reign'd but two Years; he had built his Triumphal Arch with fine Engravings, and a stately Place, with the famous Statue of *Laocoon* of one Stone, and died A. D. 79.

*Domitian* succeeded Brother *Titus*, and rebuilt the Temple of *Jupiter Capitolinus* most magnificent, overlaid it with Plates of Gold, and had all the Columns cut at *Athens*.

*Domitian* built also the Temple of *Minerva*, and that of *Flavius*; and raised a Palace more grand and rich than that of *Augustus*, with stately Galleries in the Portico, besides Halls, Baths, and beautiful Apartments for his Women. He died A. D. 93, succeeded by *Nerva*, who died 95, after he had adopted

*Trajan*, whose Warden was *Apollodorus*, the Architect, he laid his wonderful Bridge over the *Danube*, built his noble *Circus* and Palace, his two Triumphal Arches, the one at *Acona*, still standing, and the other at *Rome*, afterwards pull'd to Pieces to adorn the Arch of *Constantin*. Besides, *Trajan* erected his famous Column, a Pattern of the Kind, well known to all Connoisseurs. He died A. D. 114.

*Adrian* succeeded, a learned Designer, and even a dexterous Operator, repair'd all the publick Edifices, like a Wise *Grand-Master*, built *Adrian*'s Wall in *Britain*, his commodious Bridge at *Rome*, and his famous *Mausoleum*, or *Moles Adriani*, with accurate Collonading, and died A. D. 135.

*Antonius Pius* rais'd his curious Column, and died A. D 159.

*Marcus Aurelius* countenanc'd the Artists till he died, A. D. 178.

*Commodus*, tho' educated a Designer, turn'd vicious; and, in his Time, Painting and Sculpture began to decline at *Rome*,; tho' not yet Architecture. He died A. D. 191.

*Severus* built his *Corinthian Epizone* at *Rome*, and *Murfever* in *Britain* He died at *York*, A. D. 209.

*Coracalla* erected his splendid *Circus*, and died A. D. 215. Nor find we much more till

*Constantin* the Great, who commenc'd in *Britain* Emperor of *Rome*, A. D. 306. He repaired and beautified *Jerusalem*, *Drepanum*, *Troy*, *Chalcedon*, *Thessalonica*, &c. and rear'd at *Rome* the last Triumphal Arch in the *Augustan* Stile.

For he remov'd his Throne from *Rome* to *Bizantium*, which he call'd now *Constantinople*, and carried off all the portable Monuments of Art from *Italy*, and the best Artists to embellish his new Metropolis [\*], where he built, at a vast Rate, many artful Piles, Forums, Hippodroms, Temples or Churches, Porticoes, Fountains, a stately Imperial Palace and Senate-house, a Pillar of Porphyre of eight Stones, about 87

---

[\*] See *Petrus Gyllius* his Antiquities of *Constantinople*, translated into *English* by Mr. *Ball*, A D, 1729.

Foot

Foot high above the Pedestal, and the amazing Serpentin Pillar with his own Equestrian Statue, &c. He died A. D. 336.

*Constans* brought with him to *Rome* the famous Architect *Hormisdas*, the King of *Persia*'s Son, who was justly astonish'd at the antient Structures and Statues, and declar'd them inimitable: For now all the Arts of Designing dwindled at *Rome*, as they flourish'd at *Constantinople*. Nay the Christians, in Zeal against Heathen Idolatry, demolish'd many curious Things; till

The *Roman* Empire partition'd between two Brothers, *viz. Valentinian* I. Emperor of the West at *Rome*. Now the Christians at *Rome* adorn'd their old Church of St. *Peter*'s with the Columns of *Adrian*'s Mole, but could not follow the just Proportions of the Antients. He died A. D. 374. and this Empire was soon engross'd by the Eastern; and *Valens* Emperor of the East at *Constantinople*, who was distress'd by the *Goths*, and died without Issue, A. D. 378.

*Theodosius* the Great succeeded, who built a fine Column like that of *Trajan*, with his Brazen Statue on the Top of it, and a great *Circus*.

*Theodosius* gloried in being the Patron of all the Designers and Operators (the same as *Grand-Master*) and loved them so well, that, by a Law, he exempted all the Craft from Taxation.

The Northern Nations of *Europe*, the *Goths, Vandals, Huns, Allemans, Herules, Sweves, Dacians, Alans, Franks, Gepidans, Saxons, Angles, Longobards*, and many more, had gradually grown powerful as the *Roman* Empire decay'd; and invaded *Greece, Asia, Gaul, Spain*, and *Africa*, nay *Italy* itself; Over-running the polite World like a Deluge, with warlike Rage and gross Ignorance, the Enemies of Arts and Sciences.

But *Theodosius* stop'd their Carreer, became sole Emperor of the East and West, and died A. D. 395.

*Theodosius*

*Theodosius* divided the Empire between his two Sons, *viz.*

1. *Honorius* Emperor of the West at *Rome*, in whose Reign *Alaricus* the warlike *Visogoth* took in *Rome*, A. D. 409. *Honorius* died A. D. 423.

*Valentinian* III. succeeded, in whose Reign *Attila* the *Hun* laid *Italy* waste, and would have destroy'd *Rome*, but for the Prudence of the Bishop. When he died 455. Ten nominal Emperors succeeded. Mean while *Gensericus* the *Vandal* came from *Carthage*, and plunder'd *Rome*, 456.

At last *Augustulus*, the Tenth of those nominal Emperors, fairly abdicated for fear of *Odoacer* King of the *Herules*, 475. So ended the Western Empire. When the *Gothic* Kings of *Italy* succeeded, *viz.* *Odoacer* King of *Italy* reign'd 17 Years, till slain by *Theodoric* the *Goth*. A. D. 492. He, and his Race, reign'd Kings of *Italy* during 48 Years, till A. D. 540, when *Totila* was elected King of *Italy*. But maliciously designing to extinguish the Name and Memorial of old *Rome*, *Totila* set it on fire during 13 Days, and had demolished about two Thirds of that lofty Metropolis of the World, before he was beat off by *Bellisarius*, A. D. 547.------O *Gothic* Ignorance!

And here we may date the total Departure of the *Augustan* Stile in *Italy* and the West. See its Revival in the next Chapter.

2. *Arcadius* Emperor of the East at *Constantinople*, who inriched that City with many fine Structures, and his lofty Pillar, with a Stair in the Heart of it, 147 Foot high. He died A. D. 408.

*Theodosius*, Junior, erected there Statues, Columns and Obelisks, the Spoils of *Greece*, *Egypt*, and *Asia*; repair'd the great Church of St. *Sophia*, and died A. D. 449.

The following Emperors of the East supported the *Lodges* or Academies, of the Artists or Craftsmen, down to *Justinian*

*Justinian* I. who began A. D. 526. He restored the whole *Roman* Empire almost to its pristine Glory, Nay, laudable for the *Augustan* Stile, he sent his General, the brave *Bellisarius*, with an Army against *Totila* the *Goth*, whom he forced to run away; and so *Bellisarius* saved as much of Old *Rome* as he could. A. D. 547.

*Justinian* I. by his General *Narses*, destroyed *Totila*, 551. He collected the *Roman* Laws in his *Codex Justinianus*; and expended 34 Millions of Gold in rebuilding the Chappel of St. *Sophia*, which he intended to be equal in Decoration to *Solomon*'s Temple, tho' in vain. When this Learned Grand-Master died, A. D. 565.

*Justin* II. succeeded, who, upon the Death of *Teyas* the last Gothic King of *Italy*, A. D. 568, appointed the Exarchs of *Ravenna* to succeed the *Roman* Consuls, to rule *Italy* by the *Roman* Laws, and to stop the Incursions of the *Longobards*; which they did, till the last Exarch was expell'd by *Luitprandus* King of *Lombardy*, A. D. 741.

The *Longobards* began to reign in the North of *Italy* (from them called *Lombardy*) the same Time with the Exarchs of *Ravenna*, till conquer'd by *Charlemain*, who captivated *Desiderius* the last King of *Lombardy*, 771.

But to return; *Justin* II. died A. D. 582. Succeeded by *Tiberius* II. and he by *Mauricus* who murder'd *Phocas*, and he was murder'd by *Heraclius*, who commenced A. D. 610. Father of *Constantin* III. Father of *Constans* II. Father of *Constantin* IV. Father of *Justinian* II. murder'd 710; when the Eastern Emperors, called the *Iconoclastes*, or Destroyers of Images, began. So that here we may date the Departure of the *Augustan* Stile from the East; after the Havock of *Totila* 163 Years.

Thus

Thus the *Augustan* Stile was quite lost, and the Loss was publick.

Now the 12th Year of *Heraclius*, A. D. 622. is the first Year of the Mahometan *Hegira*. And so if

From this Year, A. D. 1750.
We substract Years 621.

The present *Anno Hegira* is 1129.
But the grand Design of the *Mahometans* was not to cultivate Arts and Sciences, but to convert the World by Fire and Sword: So that Architecture in *Asia* and *Africa* suffered by them, as in *Europe* by the *Goths*. For when the *Gothic* Nations, and those conquer'd by them, began to affect stately Structures, they wanted both Heads and Hands to imitate the Antients; nor could they do it for many Ages (as in the next Chapter) yet not wanting Wealth and Ambition they did their best; and so the more Ingenious gradually Coalesced in Societies or *Lodges*, in Imitation of the Antients, according to the remaining Traditions that were not quite obliterated, and hammer'd out a New Stile of their own call'd the *Gothic*.

But tho' this is more expensive than the Old Stile, and discovers now to us the Ignorance of the Architect, and the Improprieties of the Edifice; yet the Inventions of the Artists, to supply the Want of good old Skill, and their costly Decorations, have manifested their great Esteem of the Royal Art, and have rendered their *Gothic* Structures venerable and magnificent; tho' not Inimitable by those that have the true, high Taste of the *Grecian* or *Augustan* Stile.

CHAP.

# CHAP. VII.

*The* REVIVAL *of* Old Architecture, *or the* Augustan *Stile.*

THE Royal Art lies dead and buried still in the East, by the wilful Ignorance of the *Mahometan* Nations. But first in *Italy*, it began to peep from under its Rubbish in *Tuscany*: For the *Pisans* brought from *Greece* a few Marble Columns and other Fragments of old *Masonry* for their new Cathedral carried on by *Buschetto* the *Greek*, who first began to imitate the Antients.

After *Totila*'s Havock, A. D. 547.
Years 466.
A. D. 1013.

He join'd with others to form a new *Lodge* for that laudable Imitation, built St. *John*'s at *Pisa*, and educated many Artists that long'd for the Revival, till *Il Buono* flourish'd at *Ravenna*, and built at *Venice* the Steeple of St. *Mark* A. D. 1152.

*Oltromontano* and *Bonnano* built the Steeple of *Pisa*, 1174.

*Marchione* of *Arezzo* rais'd the Marble Chappel of *Presepio* at St. *Mary Majore*, 1216.

*James* the *German* built the first fine Edifices of *Florence*, whose Son *Jacopo Arnolpho Lapo*, with the Painter *Cimabolus*, design'd the Cathedral of St. *Mary Delfiore*, 1298.

*Charles* of *Anjou*, King of *Naples*, was the first Prince that publickly encouraged the Revival of the Arts of Designing, by employing the said *Cimabolus* and *Nicholas Pisan* to build an Abby in the Plain of *Taglia Cozzo*, where *Charles* had defeated the Pretender *Conradin*. *John Pisan*, Son of *Nicholas*, built for the

King

King his new Castle of *Naples*. This Royal Patron, (the same as *Grand Master*) of the Revivers, died A D 1285. And his Successors inriched the Kingdom of *Naples* with learned Architects, and splendid Edifices.

*Cimabouis*, and the *Pisans*, educated many fine *Masters* and *Fellow Crafts*; particularly,

*Giotto* the Architect, till the *Florentines* arrived at a pretty good Imitation of the Antients, which was discover'd in all the Parts of the Church of St. *Miniate*.

After *Totila*'s Havock,   547.
Years,   753.
A. D. 1300.

*Giotto*, and his Pupils, form'd an Academy of Designers, or a learned *Lodge* at *Florence*, who, like those of old at *Athens* and *Sicyon*, inlightened all *Italy*, by sending forth excellent Connoisseurs and dexterous Operators in all the Arts of Designing.

*Andrew Pisan*, one of them, was made a Magistrate of *Florence*, and many of them afterwards flourished Wealthy at *Pisa*, *Ravenna*, *Venice*, *Urbino*, *Rome*, and *Naples*.

*Laurentio Ghiberto*, educated there, conducted for some Time the Raising of the said St. *Mary Delfiore*, and framed the two brazen Gates of St. *John*'s, of which, long afterwards, *Michael Angelo* said in Rapture, that they were worthy of being the Gates of *Paradise*.

*Donatello* next appear'd, with *Andrea Verrochio*, the Master of *Piedro Perrugino*, and *Leonardo da Vinci*, prodigious Men! Also *Dominigo Ghirlandaio*, the Master of *Michael Angelo* and *Maiano*, and other sublime and profound Architects.

Yet the *Gothic* Stile was not quite left off at *Florence*, till

*Brunelefchi*, having studied at *Rome* the Beauty and Accuracy of the old *Roman* Buildings there standing or prostrate, return'd full fraught to *Florence*, where
he

( 67 )

he establish'd the ample and compleat Use of the *Doric*, *Ionic*, *Corinthian* and *Composite* Orders, and so the *Gothic* Stile was wholly laid aside there, and the *Augustan* Stile was entirely reviv'd

After *Totila*'s Havock, 547.
Years just 853.
A. D. 1400.

This happy Revival was also much owing to the Countenance and Encouragement given to the Learned, by the Princes of the House of *Medicis*. Thus

1. *John de Medicis*, Duke of *Florence*, became the learned Patron of the Revivers, or their *Grand Master*, and carefully supported the said *Lodge*, or Academy of Masters and Connoisseurs, at *Florence*, till he died, A. D. 1428.

2. *Cosmo* I. *de Medicis*, educated in that same Academy, succeeded his Father as Duke of *Florence*, and *Grand Master* of the Revivers. He erected a fine Library of the best Manuscripts brought from *Greece* and *Asia*, and a curious Cabinet of the rarest and most valuable Things that could be gather'd. He establish'd very great Commerce by Sea and Land, and justly acquir'd the Title of *Pater Patriæ*, the Father of his Country, and died A. D. 1464.

3 *Peter* I. *de Medicis* upheld the Lodge, and died Duke of *Florence*, A. D. 1472. But he was not so eminent as either his Father or his Son.

4. *Laurentio* I. *de Medicis* Duke of *Florence*, stiled the *Magnificent*, was both *Horace* and *Mecænas*, and *Grand Master* of the Revivers. He inriched his Grandfather's Library and Cabinet at a vast Expence; and erected a great Gallery in his Garden for educating the more promising Youth, among whom young *Michael Angelo*, as a Favourite, was admitted to the Duke's Table. This kind *Grand Master* died 9 *Apr* 1492.

---

*Laurentio de* **Medicis**, a Lord in *Florence*, slain 1474.

5 *Peter*

5. *Peter* II. *de Medicis* succeeded Duke of *Florence*, upheld his Father's curious Works, and countenanced the Accademies and *Lodges*, till he died 1504.

*John de Medicis* was elected Pope *Leo* X. 1513, a zealous Patron of the Revivers at *Rome*, especially in carrying on the gorgeous Cathedral of St. *Peters*, till he died, A. D. 1521.

By his Wife Duke *Peter* had

6. *Laurentio* II. *de Medicis* succeeded his Father 1504, Duke of *Florence*, and Patron of the Revivers, till he died without Issue, 1519.

By his Mistress Duke *Peter* had

7. *Alexander de Medicis*, who succeeded *Laurentio* as Duke of *Florence*, 1519, and by the Emperor *Charles* V. was made the first absolute Duke, A. D. 1531. He patroniz'd the Designers and Operators, till he died without Issue, A. D. 1537.

*Lewis*, or *John de Medicis*.

8. *Cosmo* II. *de Medicis*, succeeded Duke *Alexander* 1537, as absolute Duke of *Florence*. He instituted the Knights of the Order of St. *Stephen*, 1561. Pope *Pius* V, and the Emperor *Ferdinand* I, gave him the Title of *Great Duke* of *Tuscany*, A. D. 1569.

He was the chief Patron, or *Grand Master*, of all the *Italian* Designers and Craftsmen in Architecture, Painting, Sculpture, Statuary, Carving and Plaster-

---

*John Julian de Medicis*, the most beautiful Youth, and the most excellent Connoisseur in true old Architecture in all *Florence*. This *John Julian* was also a dexterous Operator, to the great Honour of the Fellow Crafts. He died 1498.

*Lewis*, call'd *John de Medicis*, was educated at *Florence* in Mathematical Learning: But his Genius was for War, and so affected the military Architecture. He died 1526.

*Julian de Medicis*, slain 1478, whose Natural Son, *Julius de Medici*, was elected Pope *Clement* VII 1523. He was besieged by *Charles* V, and forced the *Florentines* to submit to his kinsman Duke *Alexander*, 1531. He was a most ingenious Architect, and carried on St. *Peter's* at *Rome*, till he died, 1534.

ing.

ing. He inftituted the famous Academy, or *Lodge*, at *Pifa*, for the Improvement of Difciples and Enter'd Prentices. He made fuch beautiful Alterations in the Buildings of *Florence*, that, like *Auguftus* when a dying, he faid, " I found the City built of Brick " and courfe Stone, but I leave It built of polifh'd " Marble." He died aged only 55 Years, A. D. 1574. So much for the Revivers of the Art, in the Houfe of *Medicis*. But to return.

After the Revival of the *Auguftan* Stile in *Italy*, A. D. 1400.

*Leon Baptifta Alberti* was the firft Modern that wrote of Architecture, and many excellent *Mafons* flourifh'd in this 15th Century; but more were born and educated, that prov'd the Wonders of the World in the next Century, and will be ever mention'd in the *Lodges* with the greateft Honour, for improving the Revival, as if the *Auguftan* Age it felf had revived, under the generous Encouragement of the Popes, the Princes and States of *Italy*, the Patrons of the many Lodges then conftituted. Thus

*Bramante*, the learned Monk of *Urbino*, ftudied *Mafonry* at *Milan* under *Cæfariano*; and after having narrowly examin'd all the Remains of the Antients throughout *Italy*, he was employ'd by three fucceffive Popes to build at *Rome* the Cloifter of the Church of *Peace*, the Palace of the *Chancery*, and St. *Laurence* in *Damafo*. He adorned many old Churches with Frontifpieces of his own Defigning, built the pretty little St. *Peters* in *Monto Orio*, rais'd fome Buildings in the *Vatican*, and in the Palace of *Belvidere*.

Pope *Julius* II. the learned Patron, or *Grand Mafter* of *Rome*, retain'd *Bramante* as his Architect and Grand Warden, 1503; and order'd him, as Mafter of Work, to draw the grand Defign of St. *Peters* new Cathedral in *Rome*, the largeft and moft accurate Temple now in all the Earth. And the faid Pope,

with

with *Bramante*, led a solemn Assembly of Cardinals, Clergymen, and Craftsmen, to level the Foot-Stone of Great St. *Peter*'s in due Form, A D. 1507.

*Bramante* conducted that Work 7 Years, till he died, and was buried in it by Pope *Leo* X, duly attended by his Craftsmen, A. D. 1514.

*Raphael* of *Urbino*, the Prince of Painters, had learn'd *Masonry* of his Uncle *Bramante*, and succeeded him in surveying St. *Peter*'s, till he died, aged only 37 Years, on his Birth-day, 6 *April* 1520, when he was to be made a Cardinal by Pope *Leo* X; and, with a universal Mourning, was buried in the *Rotunda Pantheon*.

*Jocunde* of *Verona*, and *Antony San Gallo*, succeeded *Raphael* at St. *Peter*'s, till they died, A D. 1535. when Pope *Paul* III preferr'd to that Office

*Michael Angelo*, the greatest Designer of his Time, and in his last Years the greatest Architect, who finding fault with *San Gallo*'s Draughts, made a new Model of St. *Peter*'s, according to which that lofty Temple was finish'd.

This *Grand-Master*, leaving his Warden *Pirro Ligorio* at St. *Peter*'s, erected the new *Capitolium*, the Palace of *Farnese*, and other accurate Structures. He had before built the *Mausoleum* in St. *Peter*'s ad *Vincula*, with the curious Statue of *Moses*, the fine Front of St. *Laurence* at *Florence*, by Order of Pope *Leo* X, the Sepulchre of the House of *Medicis*, by Order of Duke *Alexander*, and the Apostolical Chamber at *Rome*.

*Michael Angelo* certainly carried on *Masonry* to its highest Perfection, till he died at *Rome*, aged 90 Years, on 17 *Feb.* 1564, highly esteemed by all the Princes of *Europe*; and *Cosmo*, the Great Duke of *Tuscany*, stole his Corps from *Rome*, resolving that since he could not have *Angelo* alive, he wou'd have him dead, and solemnly buried him in St. *Cross* at *Flo-*

*ierce*, attended by the Fraternity, and order'd *Vasario* to design his Tomb inrich'd with the three great Marble Statues of Architecture, Painting and Sculpture.

*James Barotzi da Vignola*, succeeded *Michael Angelo* at St. *Peter*'s, by Order of Pope *Paul* V; but *Ligorio* the Grand Warden, for altering *Angelo*'s Design, was turn'd out by Pope *Gregory* XIII. *Vignola*, beside his accurate Edifices at *Rome*, and elsewhere, design'd, for *Philip* II, King of *Spain*, the famous Escurial, and St *Laurence*, Master-pieces of Art. He published a Book of the Orders, and the Beauty of his Profiles is much admired. He designed the Church of *Jesus* at *Rome*, the Castle of *Caprarola*, and the Side of the Palace of *Farnese* that is next the *Tiber*; and died at *Rome*, aged 66, A. D. 1573.

*Maderni* succeeded *Vignola* at St. *Peter*'s, and built the stately Frontispiece of that vast Temple, about the Time that Pope *Gregory* 13th made a New Calendar, or began the *New Stile*, called from him the *Gregorian*, the first Year of which is, A. D. 1582. *Gregory* dying 1585, was succeeded by Pope *Sextus Quintus*, who employ'd

*Dominico Fontana* in many curious Buildings, and to move the *Egyptian Obelisks* into publick Places Erect. After which, *Fontana* was chief Engineer of *Naples*, and built the magnificent Palace of the Vice-roy.

'Tis endless to mention the ingenious Cotemporaries of those great Masters, the other accurate Revivers and Improvers of the Royal Art; such as

*Baldessare Peruzzi*, who designed and made the Model of the Palace of *Chighi*, and his Disciple *Sebastian Serglio*.------*Julio Romano*, the chief Disciple of *Raphael*, built for the Duke of *Mantua* his Palace of *Delta*,------*Lombard* of *Milan*------*James Sansovino*, recommended by Pope *Leo* X to the *Venetians*------

*Jerom*

*Jerom Genga* built for Duke *Guido Baldo* his Palaces at *Urbino* and *Pesaro*.--------*Pellegrino Tibaldi* built the great Church of *Milan*, and its Dome was made by *John James de la Porta*-----Sir *Baccio Bandinelli*, who was knighted by Pope *Clement* VII for being a most excellent Sculptor.-------*Benvenuto Cellini*-----*Daniel de Volterra* built pretty St. *Helens* in the great Church of *Trinity del Monte* at *Rome*.-------*Perrin del Vaga* built at *Genoa* the grand Palace of Prince *Doria*, and was an inimitable Plasterer; a fine Art then much in Request.

At *Venice* also the Revival was carried on; for *Jocunde* of *Verona*, above-mention'd, built the Stone Bridge, and erected the stately Gates of *Verona*.

When *Charles* V besieged *Rome*, 1525, *Michael Angelo* retired to *Venice*, when the *Doge* got him to design the famous Bridge of *Realto*.

*James Sansovino* constituted a *Lodge* of Architects, or Masters, at *Venice*, artfully supported the Dome of St. *Mark* then in Danger\*, em- *1527 bellish'd the Palace and Treasury, and fortify'd the whole Republick as *Grand-Master of Masons*.

But at *Venice* the *Augustan* Stile was also well improv'd, by the learned *Vincent Scamotzi*, *Daniel Barbaro*, and the Great *ANDREA PALLADIO*.

*Palladio*'s excellent Genius was highly discover'd by the sacred Edifices, the Palaces, and Seats of Pleasure, and the other charming Buildings of his, throughout the State of *Venice*. He wrote also with great Judgment of the Orders of Old Architecture, and of the Temples of the Antients; which is a noble Monument of his Merit, useful to all Ages. He died renowned, A. D. 1580.

Thus *Italy* was again the Mistress of the World: not for Imperial Power, but for the Arts of Designing reviv'd from *Gothic* Rubbish.

But

But from the first Revival, the *Masons* began to form new *Lodges* (called by the Painters, Academies, or Schools, as all true *Lodges* ought to be) far more elegant than the former *Gothic Lodges*; for instructing Disciples or Enter'd Prentices, for preserving the Secrets of the Fraternity from Strangers and *Cowans*, and for improving the Royal Art, under the Patronage of the Popes, and the *Italian* Princes and States, as can be more amply proved.

# PART II.

*The History of* MASONRY *in* BRITAIN, *from* JULIUS CÆSAR, *till the Union of the* Crowns, 1603.

## CHAP. I.

*From* JULIUS CÆSAR, *to the First Arrival of the* SAXONS *in* Britain.

HISTORY fails to tell, how long the *Europeans*, in the North and West, had lost their Original Skill brought from *Shinar*, before the *Roman* Conquest: But leaving our Brother *Masons* of other Nations to deduce their History of the Royal Art in their own Manner, we shall carry on our Deduction in the *Britannic* Isles.

*Cæsar*, in his Commentaries, gives us the first certain Account of *Britain*. He landed at *Dover* on the 20th of *August*, and next Year he reached *London*, but pursued not his Conquests, because of his Design to be the *Grand Master* of the *Roman* Republick. A. M. 3949 B. C. Æ. 55 B. C. 51 Yet the *Romans* did not follow his Tract during about 97 Years; even till

*Aulus Plautius* came from the Emperor *Claudius*, A. D. 42. Next Year *Claudius* came himself; and afterwards he sent *Ostorius Scapula*, who was succeeded by several *Roman* Lieutenants, that soon formed *Lodges* for building Castles and other Forts to secure their Conquests, till the Emperor *Vespasian* sent his brave Lieutenant, about A. D. 77, *viz.*

*Julius*

*Julius Agricola*, who conquer'd as far as the Isthmus, between the Firths of *Clyde* and *Forth*, which he fortify'd by a Wall of Earth against the *Northerns*; but after he was recalled, the *Northerns* got over the Wall, and made bold Incursions into the South; till

*Adrian* the Emperor came himself, A. D. 120, and finding the War tedious and hazardous, rather chose to fence the *Roman* Province by a Rampart from *Tine Mouth* to *Solway Firth*. But afterwards *Antonius Pius* sent.

*Lollius Urbicus*, who subdued the *Brigantes*, and repuls'd the *Northerns*, even beyond *Agricola*'s Wall, which he fortified with Castles, A. D. 131.

After this we read of *Lud*, or *Lucius*, a *British* King under the *Romans*, who became Christian, and built Churches; while the War was carried on in the North with various Success, till the *Northerns* forced *Verius Lupus* to purchase Peace with a great Sum of Money. This inraged the Emperor *viz.*

*Septimius Severus*, who came with a great Army, A. D. 207, vowing to extirpate them, but could not, even tho' he penetrated to the Northern Sea; and having lost 50,000 Men in the Expedition, he was forc'd to imitate *Adrian*, and rais'd his old Rampart into a Stone Wall, call'd of old *Mur Sever*, or Wall of *Severus*; also *Greme's Dyke*, or *Picts Wall*.

When *Nonnius Philippius*, A. D. 238, came from the Emperor *Gordian*, *Emillus Crispinus*, his Master of Horse, a fine Architect, built a pretty Temple near *Carlisle*, the Altar Stone of which was lately found there, near old *Mur Sever*.

The South *Britains* had been long softened in their Manners by the *Romans*, and affected their Politeness, wearing the *Roman* Dress, and speaking *Latin*; and abounding in all Commerce, they improved in Arts and Sciences, and the *Roman* Conquest was a great Blessing to the conquer'd; beholding with Pleasure

( 76 )

their Country, formerly all Grotesque and wild, now adorned with venerable Temples, solemn Courts of Justice, stately Palaces and Mansions, large and beautiful Cities, regular Forts and Castles, convenient Bridges &c.

The joint Emperors, *Dioclesian* and *Maximian*, employ'd *Carausius* as their Admiral against the *Saxon* Pirates, who being at Peace with the *Picts*, and gaining the Army, put on the Purple, and was own'd by the other two. A. D 287

*Carausius* encouraged the Craft, particularly at *Verulam* (now St. *Albans*, *Hertfordshire*) by the worthy Knight, *Albanus*, who afterwards turn'd Christian, and was called St. *Alban*, (the Proto-Martyr in *Britain* under the *Dioclesian* Persecution) who *Carausius* em-
" ploy'd * (as the old Constitutions affirm) to invi-
" ron that City with a Stone Wall, and to build him
" a fine Palace; for which that *British* King made
" St. *Alban* the Steward of his Houshold, and chief
" Ruler of the Realm.

" St *Alban* loved *Masons* well, and cherished them
" much; and he made their Pay right good, *viz*. Two
" Shillings *per* Week, and three Pence to their Cheer;
" whereas before that Time, through all the Land, a
" Mason had but a Penny a Day and his Meat, un-
" til St. *Alban* amended it. He also obtained of the
" King a Charter for the *Free-Masons*, for to hold a
" general Council, and gave it the Name of As-
" sembly, and was thereat himself as *Grand Master*,
" and helped to make *Masons*, and gave them good
" Charges, &c."

When *Dioclesian* and *Maximinian* abdicated, A. D. 303.

*Constantius Chlorus* succeeded Emperor of the West,

---

* This is asserted by all the old Copies of the Constitutions, and the old *English Masons* firmly believed it.

a Lover

a Lover of Arts and Sciences, and much encouraged the Craft, till he died at *York*, A. D. 306, the same Year that his *British* Empress *Helena* girt *London* with a Stone Wall.

*Constantin* the Great, their Son, born in *Britain*, succeeded, who partition'd South *Britain* into four Provinces. During his Reign the Christian Religion flourish'd, the *Britains* enjoy'd Peace and Plenty, and old *Roman* Masonry appear'd in many stately and curious Piles, till he died A. D. 336.

After which the *Northerns*, joining the *Saxon* Pirates, invaded the South, till 367, till *Theodosius* (Father of the Emperor *Theodosius* the Great) came from the Emperor *Valentinian* I, and bravely beat them back, even over *Agricola*'s Wall, which he fortified with new Castles and Forts; and recovering the Land of the *Old Meats* between the two Walls, he made it a fifth Province, calling it *Valentia*. He also beautified *London*, repaired all the Cities and Forts, and left *Britain* A. D. 374.

*Maximus* (called the Tyrant) came next from the Emperor *Gratian*, who put on the Purple, sail'd into *Gaul*, but was defeated in *Italy* by *Theodosius Magnus*, and beheaded A. D. 388.

*Constantin* a common Soldier, for the Sake of his fortunate Name, was chosen by the *Southerns* to be their Leader, who also put on the Purple, sail'd into *Gaul*, and was there defeated and beheaded by the Emperor *Honorius*. And now

*Honorius*, not being able to protect the *Southerns* against the *Northerns*, fairly renounc'd his Sovereignty over *Britain*, the next Year after *Alaric* had took in *Rome*, viz. A. D. 410. Yet

*Ætius*, the General of *Valentinian* III, being victorious in *Gaul*, from Pity, sent the *Britons* one Legion under *Gallio*, who repell'd the *Northerns* beyond *Mur Sever*, which he rebuilt of Stone-work, 8 Foot broad,

and

and 12 Foot high; and being recall'd, he left the *South Britons* to defend themselves against the *Northerns*, and carried off his Legion, A. D. 426. Tho' the *Roman* Soldiers did not all depart till A. D. 430.

   In the Vulgar Year of *Masonry*,  4430.
   After *Cæsar*'s Invasion, Years  486.
   After *Aulus Plautius* came  389.

 During which Time, the *Romans* had propagated *Masonry* in every Garrison, and had built fine Places past Number, even to the North Border, or the Wall of *Agricola*; near which, at the *Forth*, they raised their little Temple of their God *Terminus*, that stands to this Day; now call'd, by the Vulgar, *Arthur's Oven*, a curious *Rotunda* in Shape of the *Pantheon* at *Rome*, 20 Foot high, and near 20 Foot in Diameter. Nay, in Times of Peace, the *Northerns* might learn of the *Romans* to extend the Art to the farthest North and West, or the *Ultima Thule*.

 But true, old *Masonry* departed also from *Britain* with the *Roman* Legions. For tho' many *Roman* Families had settled in the South, and were blended with the *Britons*, who had been well educated in the Science and the Art; yet the subsequent Wars, Confusions and Revolutions in the Island, ruined ancient Learning, till all the fine Artists were dead without Succession.

 For the *Northerns*, hearing that the *Roman* Legions were never to return, broke through *Mur Sever*, seized all the Land North of the *Humber*, and ravag'd the South the more easily, that the *Southerns* were divided by petty Kings, till they chose a general Monarch, *viz.* A. D. 445.

 *Vortigern*, who being unable to retrieve Affairs, got the Consent of his Nobles to invite the *Saxons* in Lower *Germany* to come over and help him; and so Prince *Hengist*, with 2,000 *Saxons*, landed in *Thanet* upon *Kent*, A. D. 449.

           C H A P.

## CHAP. II.

*From the first Arrival of the* Saxons, *to* William *the* Conqueror.

THE *Saxons* having assisted *Vortigern* to repulse the *Scots* and *Picts* beyond the *Humber*, built *Thong* Castle in *Lincolnshire*; and being daily recruited from Lower *Germany*, and the River *Elbe*, they resolv'd to settle here, and after much Bloodshed in many Battles between the *Britons* and *Saxons*, they founded and established their Heptarchy, or Seven Kingdoms, *viz*.

1. Kingdom of *Kent* founded by *Hengist*, A.D. 455.
2. Kingdom of *Sussex* by *Ella*, 491.
3. Kingdom of *Wessex* by *Cherdick*, 519.
4. Kingdom of *Essex* by *Erchenwyne*, 527.
5. Kingdom of *Northumbria* by *Ida* the *Angle*, 547.
6. Kingdom of *East Angles* by *Uffa*, 571.
7. Kingdom of *Middle Angles*, or *Mercia*, by *Crida*, 584.

And as the *Anglo-Saxons* increas'd, the *Britons* lost Ground, till after the Death of *Ambrosius Aurelius*, and his brave Son King *Arthur*, the *Britons* had no Grand Monarch, but only a few petty Kings: But after *Crida* landed, many of them submitted to him, (as to other *Saxon* Kings) many fled to *Cornwal*, and by Sea to *Armorica*, (called still *Britagne* in *France*) and many went to *North Britain* among the *Scoto-Wallenses*; tho' the greater Part fled beyond the *Severn*, where they were coop'd in between the Mountains and the *Irish* Sea. A. D. 589.

The *Anglo-Saxons*, who had always called the *Britons Gualish*, or *Walishmen*, now called their Settlement beyond the *Severn Walishland*, or *Wales*, called still,

still, from the *French*, *Galles*, from the *Gauls* their Progenitors. And here they elected the noble *Cadwan* their King, the Progenitor of the Christian Kings and Princes of *Wales*.

During the horrid Wars, since the Departure of the *Roman* Legions about 160 Years, *Masonry* was extinguish'd; nor have we any Vestige of it, unless we reckon that of *Stone-Heng*, and allow, with some, that *Ambrosius*, King of the *Britons*, rais'd that famous Monument on *Salisbury* Plain by the Art of marvellous *Merlin* (whom the Populace accounted a Conjuror and Prophet) in Remembrance of the bloody Congress, when *Hengist* murder'd 300 *British* Nobles. Others think it an old *Celtic* Temple built by the *Britons* long before the *Romans* came here; and some have counted it only a *Danish* Monument. But the great *Inigo Jones*,[*] and his Kinsman Mr. *John Webb*, have learnedly prov'd it to be a *Roman* Temple, the largest Piece of Antiquity in the Island.

The *Anglo-Saxons* came over all rough, ignorant Heathens, despising every thing but War; nay, in Hatred to the *Britons* and *Romans*, they demolish'd all accurate Structures, and all the glorious Remains of antient Learning, affecting only their own barbarous Manner of Life, till they became Christians; as appears from *Bede*, the *Saxon* Annals, and other good Vouchers; therefore we have no Account of *Masonry* in their first Settlements.

But where the *Welch* dwelt, we find the earliest Accounts, at least, of sacred Architecture, as at *Glastonbury* in *Devonshire*, *Paastow* in *Cornwal*; *Caerleon* or *Chester*, afterwards translated to St. *Asaph*'s in *Flintshire*; *Llan Twit*, or Church of *Iltutus*; *Llan Badarn Vawr*, or Church of Great St. *Patern*; the

---

[*] See *Stone-Heng* restor'd.

the

Monaſtry of *Llan Carvan*, *Bangor* in *Caernarvonſhire*; *Holy-head* in *Angleſey*, *Llandaff* in *Glamorganſhire*; *Menevia*, or *St. David's* in *Pembrokeſhire*; and many more Churches, Monaſtries, and Schools of Learning.

Some pious Teachers came from *Wales* and *Scotland*, and converted many of the *Anglo-Saxons* to Chriſtianity; but none of their Kings till A. D. 579, when *Auſtin*, and forty more Monks, came from Pope *Gregory* I, and baptized *Ethelbert* King of *Kent*; and in about 60 Years, all the Kings of the Heptarchy were baptized.

Then affecting to build Churches and Monaſtries, Palaces and fine Manſions, they too late repented the ignorant and deſtructive Conduct of their Fathers; but knew not how to repair the publick Loſs of old Architecture: Yet, being zealous, they follow'd the *Gothic* Stile, then only uſed, and ſoon rear'd the Cathedral of *Canterbury*, A. D. 600. That of *Rocheſter*, 602. St. *Paul's*, *London*, 604. St *Peter's Weſtminſter*, 605. And a great many more deſcribed in the *Monaſticon Anglicanum*.

They alſo built many Palaces and Caſtles; and fortified their Cities; eſpecially on the Borders of each Kingdom. This required many *Maſons*, who ſoon formed themſelves into Societies, or *Lodges*, by Direction of Foreigners who came over to help them.

Theſe many *Saxon Lodges* gradually improv'd, till *Ethelbert* King of *Mercia*, and General Monarch, ſent to *Charles Martel*, the Right Worſhipful *Grand-Maſter* of *France*, (Father of King *Pippin*) who had been educated by Brother *Mimus Græcus*: He ſent over from *France* (about A. D. 710) ſome expert *Maſons* to teach the *Saxons* thoſe Laws and Uſages of the antient Fraternity that had happily been preſerv'd from the Havock of the *Goths*; tho' not the *Auguſtan* Stile, that had been long loſt in the Weſt, and now alſo in the Eaſt. This is ſtrongly aſſerted in all the

I. old

old Conſtitutions, and was firmly believed by the old *Engliſh Maſons*.

The Clergy now found it convenient to ſtudy Geometry, and Architecture, ſuch as it was; becauſe the Noble and Wealthy, nay Kings and Queens, thought it meritorious to build Churches, and other pious Houſes, where ſome of them ended their Days in ſweet Retirement; for thoſe holy Houſes were all under the Direction of the Clergy; and the *Lodges* were held in Monaſtries before the Inundation of the *Danes*; yet they at firſt built moſtly of Timber only, till

*Bennet*, the Abbot of *Wirral*, introduced the Uſe of Brick and Stone, about A. D. 680; ſo that even the *Gothic* Stile was but in its Infancy during the Heptarchy, which laſted from *Hengiſt*'s Arrival, A. D. 449, during 381 Years, *viz.* A. D. 830. At laſt,

*Egbert*, King of *Weſſex*, by Policy and Conqueſt, became Sovereign of the other Six Kingdoms, and the *Angles* being numerous, he called his united Kingdom *England*, and all the People *Engliſhmen*. Tho' the *Welſh*, the *Iriſh*, and *Scots Highlanders*, call them ſtill *Saxons*, after thoſe that firſt came with *Hengiſt*. Thus

1 *Egbert*, the firſt King of all *England*, A. D. 830, fortified his Sea-ports, and died A. D. 836.

2. *Ethelwolth* employ'd St. *Swithin* to repair the pious Houſes, and died A. D. 857.

3. *Ethelbald* died 860.

4. *Ethelbert* died 866.

5. *Ethelred* died 872.

In whoſe Reigns the *Danes* ſettled in Eaſt *Anglia*, and *Northumbria*, pillaging and demoliſhing the pious Houſes.

6. *Alfred* the Great, the fourth Son, who commenced A. D. 872, ſubdu'd the *Danes*, tho not expell'd them. He increaſed his Navy Royal, fortified and rebuilt many Towns, and founded the Univerſity of *Oxford*.

King *Alfred* had about him the best Architects, and employ'd the Fellow-Crafts wholly in Brick or Stone. The best King of *England*, and died illustrious, A. D. 900.

7 *Edward*, Senior, left *Masonry* to the Care, first of *Ethred*, the Deputy King of *Mercia*, the Husband of *Edward*'s Sister *Elfreda*, the glorious Heroine, who by her Valour expell'd the *Danes* out of *Mercia*, and fortified many Towns and Castles to prevent their Incursions. Next the King put his learned Brother *Ethelwald* at the Head of the Fraternity, and founded the University of *Cambridge*, that had been long a Nursery of the Learned. The King died 924, leaving 3 Kings and a Queen.

8. *Athelstan*, the eldest Son, succeeded, tho' only the Son of a Concubine, and, at first, left the *Craft* to to the Care of his Brother *Edwin*, call'd, in some Copies, his Son. For in all the old Constitutions it is written to this Purpose. *viz.*

" That tho' the ancient Records of the Brother-
" hood in *England*, were most of them destroy'd or
" lost in the Wars with the *Danes*, who burnt the
" Monastries where the Records were kept; yet King
" *Athelstan* (the Grandson of King *Alfred*) the first
" annointed King of *England*, who translated the
" Holy Bible into the *Saxon* Language, when he had
" brought the Land into Rest and Peace, built many
" great Works, and encouraged many *Masons* from
" *France* and elsewhere, whom he appointed Over-
" seers thereof; they brought with them the Charges
" and Regulations of the Foreign *Lodges*, and pre-
" vail'd with the King to increase the Wages.

" That Prince *Edwin*, the King's Brother, being
" taught Geometry and *Masonry*, for the Love he had
" to the Craft, and to the honourable Principles
" whereon it is grounded, purchased a Free Charter
" of King *Athelstan* his Brother, for the *Free-Masons*

" having

" having among themselves a Correction, or a Power
" and Freedom to regulate themselves, to amend
" what might happen amiss, and to hold an yearly
" Communication in a General Assembly.

" That accordingly Prince *Edwin* summoned all the
" *Free* and *Accepted Masons* in the Realm, to meet
" him in a Congregation at *York*, who came and
" formed the *Grand Lodge* under him as their *Grand*
" *Master*, A. D. 926.

" That they brought with them many o'd Writ-
" ings and Records of the Craft, some in *Greek*, some
" in *Latin*, some in *French*, and other Languages,
" and from the Contents thereof they fram'd the Con-
" stitution of the *English Lodges*, and made a Law for
" themselves, to preserve and observe the same in all
" Time coming, &c. &c. &c."

But good King *Edwin* died before the King (A. D. 938) without Issue, to the great Grief of the Fraternity, though his Memory is fragrant in the *Lodges*, and honourably mention'd in the old Constitutions.

Some *English* Historians say, that *Edwin* being accused of a Plot, the King set him adrift in a Boat without Sail and Oars; that *Edwin* protesting his Innocence, went aboard and jumpt into the Sea; and that his Esquire was drove into *Picardy*.

But the Historian *Malmsbury* disbelieves the whole Story, as grounded only on some old Ballad; and because of *Athelstan*'s known Kindness and Love to all his Brothers and Sisters. And *Huntindon* writes of the Loss of *Edwin* by Sea, as a very sad Accident, and a great Misfortune to *Athelstan*, who was very fond of him.

King *Athelstan* built many Castles in *Northumbria* to bridle the *Danes* (whom he had subdu'd) and the famous Abby of St. *John* at *Beverly* (lately repaired for Divine Service) and *Melton Abby* in *Dorsetshire*;

he

he rebuilt the City of *Exeter*, and repaired the old Church of the *Culdees* at *York*. He died without Issue, A. D. 940.

### *Saxon* Kings of *England*.

9. *Edmund* I. succeeded Brother *Athelstan*, repair'd the Cities and Churches, and leaving two Sons died A. D. 946.

10. *Edred* succeeded his Brother *Edmund*, re-built *Glastonbury*, and died without Issue, 955.

11. *Edwin* succeeded his Uncle *Edred*, and died without Issue, 959.

12. *Edgar* built and rebuilt about 48 pious Houses, by the Direction of St. *Dunstan*, *Grand Master*, and several more expert Masters. He rigg'd out a good Navy, which prevented the Invasions of the *Danes*, and died 975.

13. *Edward* Junior, call'd the Martyr, died without Issue, 979.

14. *Ethelred* II was always distress'd by the *Danes*, and contrived their Massacre, A D. 1002.

*Ethelred*, upon the Death of *Swen Otto*, return'd, but died inglorious, 1016.

By his first Wife he had

16. *Edmund* II, *Ironsides*, reign'd in the West, till murder'd A. D. 1017, Father of Prince *Edward*, who died at *London*, 1057.

Prince *Edgar Atheling* died without Issue.

*Margaret*, Wife of *Malcolm Keanmore* King of *Scotland*.

By his second Wife *Ethelred* had

20. *Edward* the *Confessor*, who succeeded King *Hardy Knut* in the Throne of *England*, 1041. He collected the *Saxon* Laws in a Body. In his Reign Arts and Sciences flourish'd. *Leofrick*, the wealthy Earl of *Coventry*, at the Head of the *Free-Masons*, built the Abby of *Coventry*, and others built 12 more

pious Houses. The King rebuilt *Westminster-Abby*, tho' not as it now stands, and died without Issue on the 5th of *January*, 106¾, when the Nobles and People chose

21. *Harold* II, Son of Earl *Goodwin*, who reigned nine Months; even till *William* the Bastard, the Duke of *Normandy*, slew *Harold* bravely fighting in the Battle of *Hastings* in *Sussex*, where the *English* were Totally routed by the *Normans*, on the 14th of *October*, A. D. 1066.

   In the Vulgar Year of *Masonry*  5066.
   After *Hengist*'s Arrival     617.
   After the End of the Heptarchy  236.

### *Danish* Kings of *England*.

*Thyra*, Daughter of *Edward* Senior, (according to the *Danish* Historians) was married to *Gormo* III, King of *Denmark*, and bore to him

*Harold* VIII, King of *Denmark*.

*Swen Otto*, King of *Denmark*, who finding that *Ethelred* neglected his Fleet, allow'd his *Danes* to invade *England* every Year, and they left many Lord *Danes* to oppress the poor *English*. But hearing of the Massacre, *Swen Otto* sailed over with great Force, and drove *Ethelred* into *Normandy*. And so

15. *Swen Otto* was King of *England*, 1013; but died suddenly, 1014.

17. *Canutus*, or *Knut Magnus*, after the Death of King *Edmund Ironsides*, was crown'd King of all *England*, A. D. 1017.

He built the Abby of St. *Edmund's-Bury*, and died 1036, Father of

18. *Harold* I, *Harefoot*, King of *England*, died without Issue, A. D. 1039.

19. *Hardy-Knut*, King of *England*, the last of the *Danish* Race, died without Issue, A. D. 1041.

As

he rebuilt the City of *Exeter*, and repaired the old Church of the *Culdees* at *York*. He died without Issue, A. D. 940.

### Saxon Kings of *England*.

9. *Edmund* I. succeeded Brother *Athelstan*, repair'd the Cities and Churches, and leaving two Sons died A. D. 946.

10. *Edred* succeeded his Brother *Edmund*, re-built *Glastonbury*, and died without Issue, 955.

11. *Edwin* succeeded his Uncle *Edred*, and died without Issue, 959.

12. *Edgar* built and rebuilt about 48 pious Houses, by the Direction of St. *Dunstan, Grand Master,* and several more expert Masters. He rigg'd out a good Navy, which prevented the Invasions of the *Danes*, and died 975.

13. *Edward* Junior, call'd the Martyr, died without Issue, 979.

14. *Ethelred* II was always distress'd by the *Danes*, and contrived their Massacre, A D. 1002.

*Ethelred,* upon the Death of *Swen Otto,* return'd, but died inglorious, 1016.

By his first Wife he had

16. *Edmund* II, *Ironsides,* reign'd in the West, till murder'd A. D. 1017, Father of Prince *Edward,* who died at *London*, 1057.

Prince *Edgar Atheling* died without Issue.

*Margaret,* Wife of *Malcolm Keanmore* King of *Scotland.*

By his second Wife *Ethelred* had

20. *Edward* the *Confessor,* who succeeded King *Hardy Knut* in the Throne of *England*, 1041. He collected the *Saxon* Laws in a Body. In his Reign Arts and Sciences flourish'd. *Leofrick,* the wealthy Earl of *Coventry,* at the Head of the *Free-Masons,* built the Abby of *Coventry,* and others built 12 more

pious

pious Houses. The King rebuilt *Westminster-Abby*, tho' not as it now stands, and died without Issue on the 5th of *January*, 106⅚, when the Nobles and People chose

21. *Harold* II, Son of Earl *Goodwin*, who reigned nine Months; even till *William* the Bastard, the Duke of *Normandy*, slew *Harold* bravely fighting in the Battle of *Hastings* in *Sussex*, where the *English* were Totally routed by the *Normans*, on the 14th of *October*, A. D. 1066.

   In the Vulgar Year of *Masonry*  5066.
   After *Hengist*'s Arrival     617.
   After the End of the Heptarchy  236.

### *Danish* Kings of *England*.

*Thyra*, Daughter of *Edward* Senior, (according to the *Danish* Historians) was married to *Gormo* III, King of *Denmark*, and bore to him

*Harold* VIII, King of *Denmark*.

*Swen Otto*, King of *Denmark*, who finding that *Ethelred* neglected his Fleet, allow'd his *Danes* to invade *England* every Year, and they left many Lord *Danes* to oppress the poor *English*. But hearing of the Massacre, *Swen Otto* sailed over with great Force, and drove *Ethelred* into *Normandy*. And so

15. *Swen Otto* was King of *England*, 1013; but died suddenly, 1014.

17. *Conutus*, or *Knut Magnus*, after the Death of King *Edmund Ironsides*, was crown'd King of all *England*, A. D. 1017.

He built the Abby of St. *Edmund's-Bury*, and died 1036, Father of

18. *Harold* I, *Harefoot*, King of *England*, died without Issue, A. D. 1039.

19. *Hardy-Knut*, King of *England*, the last of the *Danish* Race, died without Issue, A. D. 1041.

As for the *Danes*, having no particular Head, they had submitted to the *Saxon* Kings, and daily loosing their Genealogy, they were gradually blended with the *Anglo-Saxons*, having much the same Language.

## CHAP. III.

### Masonry *in* England *from* William *the Conqueror, to King* Henry IV.

1. WILLIAM I, the Conqueror, having settled *England*, appointed *Gundulph* Bishop of *Rochester*, *Roger de Montgomery*, Earl of *Shrewsbury* and *Arundel*, and other good Architects, to be at the Head of the Fellow-Crafts; first in Civil and Military Architecture, building for the King, the *Tower* of *London*, the Castles of *Dover*, *Exeter*, *Winchester*, *Warwick*, *Hereford*, *Stafford*, *York*, *Durham*, and *New-Castle* upon *Tyne*; whereby the proud *Normans* bridled the *English*.

Next, in sacred Architecture, building *Battle Abby* near *Hastings*, in Memory of his Conquest, *St. Saviours*, *Southwark*, and nine more pious Houses; while others built 42 such, and five Cathedrals. The King brought many expert *Masons* from *France*, and died in *Normandy*, A. D. 1087.

2. *William* II, *Rufus*, succeeded his Father, and employ'd his Architects and Craftsmen in building a new Wall round the *Tower*, and in rebuilding *London Bridge*; and, by Advice of his *Grand Lodge* of *Masters*, he built the great Palace of *Westminster*, with large *Westminster Hall*, 270 Foot long, and 74 Foot broad, the largest one Room upon Earth, and four pious Houses; while others built 28 such. He died without Issue, A. D. 1100.

3. *Henry*

3. *Henry* I, *Beau Clerc*, born at *Selby* in *Yorkshire*, succeeded Brother *William*, though the eldest Brother, *Robert* Duke of *Normandy*, was alive.

Now the *Norman* Barons perceiving their great Possessions in *England* depended on the Royal Pleasure; and finding the Laws of the *Anglo-Saxons* to be better for securing Property than the Laws of *Normandy*; the *Normans* began to call themselves *Englishmen*, to assert the *Saxon* Rights, and prevailed with this King to grant them the first *Magna Charta*, or Larger Paper, and Deeds of Rights, in this first Year of his Reign, A. D. 1100.

This King built the great Palace of *Woodstock*, and a little one at *Oxford* to converse with the Learned, and 14 pious Houses; while others built about 100 such, besides many fine Mansions. He died A. D. 1135, succeeded by his Nephew, *viz.*

4. *Stephen* Count of *Boulloign*, Son of *Adela* Daughter of *William* the Conqueror, by the Power of the Clergy, during the Civil Wars between him and *Maud* the Empress, the Nobles and Gentry being courted by both, laid hold of the Occasion to build about 1100 Castles, that prov'd afterwards very convenient for them in the *Barons* Wars, so that the *Masons* were as much employ'd as the Soldiers, under their *Grand Master Gilbert de Clare*, Marquis of *Pembroke*, by whom the King built 4 Abbies and 2 Nunneries, with St. *Stephen*'s Chapel in the Palace of *Westminster*; while others built about 90 pious Houses. King *Stephen* died without Issue Male, A. D. 1154. The last of the Royal *Normans*.

After the Conquest, Years 88.

King *Henry* I, by his Wife *Maud* (Daughter of *Malcolm Keanmore* by his Wife *Margaret* the *Saxon* Heiress of *England*) left only a Daughter, *viz.*

*Maud* the Empress, who next married *Geoffry Plantagenet* Count of *Anjou*, A. D. 1127.

She

She came over, though too late, to assert her Claim (to which her Father had sworn the whole Kingdom, even *Stephen* also) and fought like a brave Heroine; but refusing to confirm *Magna Charta*, she was deserted; and her best Friends dying, she was forc'd to return to *Anjou*, A. D. 1147. But her Son *Henry* came over and asserted his Claim, till *Stephen* agreed that *Henry* should succeed him.

Accordingly, when *Stephen* died, the *Plantagenet* of *Anjou* commenc'd, *viz.*

1 *Henry* II *Plantagenet*, Count of *Anjou*, became King of *England*, A. D. 1154, who fortified some Castles against the *Welsh* and *Scots*, built some little Palaces, and 10 pious Houses; while others built about 100 such. The *Grand Master* of the *Knights Templars* erected their Society, and built their *Temple* in *Fleetstreet*, *London*. The King died A. D. 1189.

2. *Richard* I, much abroad, died without Issue 1199; yet in this Reign about 20 pious Houses were built.

3. King *John* succeeded Brother *Richard*, and first made his Chaplain, *Peter de Cole-Church*, *Grand Master* of the *Masons* in rebuilding *London-Bridge* of Stone, which was finish'd by the next Master, *William Almain*, A. D. 1209. Next *Peter de Rupibus*, Bishop of *Winchester*, was *Grand Master*, and, under him, *Geoffry Fitz-Peter* was Chief Surveyor, or Deputy *Grand Master*, who built much for the King; while others built about 40 pious Houses. The King died A. D. 1216, succeeded by his Son

4. *Henry* III, a Minor of nine Years, when *Peter de Rupibus*, the old *Grand Master*, came to be the King's Guardian; he levelled the Foot-Stone of *Westminster Abby*, in that Part called *Solomon's Porch*, A. D. 1220.

*Peter* Count of *Savoy* (Brother of the Queen-Mother) built the Palace of *Savoy* in the *Strand*, *London*;

and *John Balliol*, Lord of *Bernard Castle* in *Durham* (Father of *John* King of *Scotland*) founded *Balliol College* in *Oxford*. The Templars built their *Domus Dei* at *Dover*, and others built 32 pious Houses. The King died A. D. 1272.

5. *Edward* I, being deeply engaged in Wars, left the Craft to the Care of several successive Grand Masters, as *Walter Gifford*, Arch-bishop of *York*, *Gilbert de Clare*, Earl of *Glocester*; and *Ralph* Lord of *Mount Hermer*, the Progenitor of the *Montagues*, and by these the King fortified many Castles, especially against the *Welch*, till they submitted to him, A. D. 1284, when *Edward*, the King's Son and Heir, was born at *Caermarthen*, the first *English* Prince of *Wales*.

The King celebrated the Cape-stone of *Westminster Abby*, A. D. 1285, just 65 Years after it was founded. But that Abby and the Palace being burnt down 1299, the King order'd the Palace to be repair'd, but was diverted from repairing the Abby by his Wars in *Scotland*. In this Reign *Merton College Oxford*, the Cathedral of *Norwich*, and about 20 more pious Houses were founded. The King died in his Camp on *Solway Sands*, 7th *July*, 1307.

6. *Edward* II made *Walter Stapleton*, Bishop of *Exeter*, Grand Master, who built *Exeter* and *Oriel* Colleges in *Oxford*; while others built *Clare-Hall Cambridge*, and 8 pious Houses. The King died A. D. 1327.

7. *Edward* III. became the Patron of Arts and Sciences. He set up a Table at *Windsor*, 600 Feet round, for feasting the gallant Knights of all Nations, and rebuilt the Castle and Palace of *Windsor*, as a Royal *Grand Master*, by his several Deputies, or Masters of Work, viz.

1. *John de Spoulee*, call'd Master of the *Ghiblim*,

who

who rebuilt St *George's Chappel*; where the King constituted the Order of the Garter, 1350.

2. *William a Wicklow*, at the Head of 400 Free-Masons, rebuilt the Castle strong and stately, A. D. 1357, and when he was made Bishop of *Winchester*, A. D. 1367. Then next

3. *Robert a Barnham* succeeded, at the Head of 250, Free-Masons, and finished St. *George's* great Hall, with other Works in the Castle, A. D. 1375.

4. *Henry Yevele* (call'd at first, in the old Records, the King's Free-Mason) built for the King, the *London Charter-house*, *King's-Hall*, *Cambridge*, *Queensborough* Castle, and rebuilt St. *Stephen's* Chapel, now the House of Commons in Parliament.

5. *Simon Langham*, Abbot of *Westminster*, who repaired the Body of that Cathedral as it now stands.

The King also founded the Abby of *Eastminster*, near the *Tower*; and his laudable Example was well followed; for the Queen endowed *Queen's College, Oxford*; while others built many stately Mansions, and about 30 pious Houses, for all the expensive Wars of this Reign.

The Constitutions were new meliorated, for an old Record imports, "That in the glorious Reign of
" King *Edward* III, when Lodges were many and
" frequent, the Grand Master, with his Wardens at
" the Head of the Grand Lodge, with consent of the
" Lords of the Realm, then generally Free-Masons,
" ordained,

" That for the future, at the Making or Admission
" of a Brother, the Constitutions shall be read, and
" the Charges hereunto annexed.

" That Master Masons, or Masters of Work, shall be
" examin'd whether they be able of Cunning to serve
" their respective Lords, as well the highest as the
" lowest, to the Honour and Worship of the foresaid
" Art, and to the Profit of their Lords; for they be
" their

" their Lords that employ and pay them for their
" Travel.

" That when the Master and Wardens preside in a
" *Lodge*, the Sheriff if need be, or the Mayor, or the
" Alderman (if a Brother) where the Chapter is held,
" shall be Sociate to the Master, in help of him
" against Rebels, and for upholding the Right of the
" Realm.

" That *Enter'd Prentices*, at their making, shall
" be charged not to be Thieves, nor Thieves Main-
" tainers. That the Fellow Crafts shall travel ho-
" nestly for their Pay, and love their Fellows as them-
" selves. and, that all shall be true to the King, to
" the Realm, and to the Lodge.

" That if any of the Fraternity shall be fractious,
" mutinous, or disobedient to the *Grand Master*'s Or-
" ders, and after proper Admonitions, shall persist in
" his Rebellion, he shall forfeit all his Claim to the
" Rights, Benefits, and Privileges of a true and faith-
" ful Brother, &c. Concluding with *Amen*. So
" mote it be."

King *Edward* III. died 21 *June*, 1377.

*Edward* the *Black Prince* of *Wales* died before his Father, A. D. 1376.

* See the other Sons, with respect to the Succession, in the Note below.

8. *Richard*

---

* The other Sons of King *Edward* III, with respect to the Succession.

*Lionel* Duke of *Clarence*, the second Son, left only

*Philippa* of *Clarence*, Wife of *Edmund Mortimer* Earl of *March*, Mother of

*Roger Mortimer* Earl of *March*, left only

*Anne Mortimer*, the Heiress of *Clarence* and *March*.

*Edmund* Duke of *York*, the fourth Son, Patriarch of the *White Rose*, by his Wife *Isabella*, second Daughter of *Piedro Crudelis*, King of *Castile*.

*Richard*

8 *Richard* II. succeeded his Grandfather A. D. 1377; he employ'd *William a Wickham*, Bishop of *Winchester*, *Grand Master*, to rebuild *Westminster-Hall* as it now stands; and *William*, at his own Cost, built *New-College, Oxford*, and founded *Winchester-College*; while others built about 15 pious Houses.

At last, while King *Richard* was in *Ireland*, his Cousin *Henry* Duke of *Lancaster* landed in *Yorkshire*, rais'd a great Army, seiz'd King *Richard* upon his Return, got the Parliament to depose him, and succeeded in the Throne, A. D. 1399; and next Year *Richard* was murder'd without Issue.

---

*Richard* Earl *Cambridge*, beheaded 1415.
*Richard* Duke of *York*, slain 1460.
King *Edward* IV,
King *Richard* III.
*John a Gaunt* Duke of *Lancaster*, the third Son, Patriarch of the *Red Rose*    Wives
  1 *Blanche* of *Lancaster*, Mother of King *Henry* IV
  2 *Constantia*, eldest Daughter of *Pedro Crudelis* King of *Castile*, Mother of *Katherine* married to *Henry* III King of *Castile*
  3 *Katherine Roet*, his Concubine, whom at last he married, and her Children were legitimated by Act of Parliament, but not to inherit the Crown.    Mother of
*John Beaufort*, (not *Plantagenet*) Earl of *Somerset*.
*John Beaufort*, Duke of *Somerset*
*Margaret Beaufort*, Mother of King *Henry* VII.

CHAP.

( 94 )

## CHAP. IV.

Masonry *in* England, *from* Henry IV, *to the* Royal Tewdors.

KING *Edward* III.

*John a Gaunt*, Duke of *Lancaster*, Patriarch of the *Red Rose*. or the Royal *Lancastrians*, by his first Wife, *Blanche* of *Lancaster*, had

6 *Henry* IV, Duke of *Lancaster*, who supplanted and succeeded King *Richard* II, A. D. 1399. He appointed *Thomas Fitz-Allen* Earl of *Surry*, to be *Grand Master*; and after his famous Victory of *Shrewsbury*, the King founded *Battle Abbey* there, and afterwards that of *Fotheringay* Others built 6 pious Houses, and the *Londoners* founded their present *Guild-hall*, a large and magnificent Fabrick. The King died 1413.

10. *Henry* V, while triumphing in *France*, ordered the Palace and Abby of *Sheen* (now call'd *Richmond* upon *Thames*) to be rebuilt, by the Direction of the Grand Master *Henry Chicherly*, Archbishop of *Canterbury*; while others built 8 pious Houses. The King died A. D. 1422.

By his Queen *Catherine* of *France* (afterwards the Wife of *Owen Tewdor*) he had

11. *Henry* VI, a Minor of nine Months, in whose third Year an ignorant Parliament endeavoured to disturb the *Lodges*, tho' in vain; by the following Act, *viz.*

3. Hen. VI. Cap. I. *A. D.* 1425.
TITLE. " *Masons* shall not Confederate in Chapters and Congregations."

" Whereas by yearly Congregations, and Confede-
" racies made by the *Masons* in their general Assem-
" blies, the good Course and Effect of the Statutes
" of

" of Labourers be openly violated and broken, in
" Subversion of the Law, and to the great Damage
" of all the Commons; Our Sovereign Lord the
" King, willing in this Case to provide a Remedy,
" by the Advice and Consent aforesaid, and at the
" special Request of the Commons, hath Ordained
" and Established,

" That such Chapters and Congregations shall not
" hereafter be holden; and if any such be made, they
" that shall cause such Chapters and Congregations
" to be assembled and holden, if they thereof be con-
" vict, shall be judged for Felons: And that other
" *Masons* who come to such Chapters and Congrega-
" tions be punished by Prisonment of their Bodies,
" and make Fine and Ransom at the King's Will."

But this Act is explain'd in Judge *Coke*'s *Institutes*, Part III. Fol. 19. where we find, that the Cause why this Offence was made Felony, is, for that the good Course and Effect of the Statutes of Labourers was thereby violated and broken. Now, says my Lord *Coke*,

' All the Statutes concerning Labourers before this
' Act, and whereunto this Act doth refer, are repeal'd
' by the 5 *Eliz*. Cap. 4. about A. D. 1562. where-
' by the Cause and End of making this Act is taken
' away, and consequently the Act is become of no
' Force; for *Cessante ratione legis cessat ipsa lex!* And
' the Inditement of Felony upon this Statute must
' contain, that those Chapters and Congregations are
' to the violating and breaking of the good Course
' and Effect of the Statutes of Labourers! which now
' cannot be so alleged, because those Statutes be re-
' pealed. Therefore this would be put out of the
' Charge of Justices of the Peace.'

But this Act was never executed, nor ever fright-ened the *Free-Masons* from holding their Chapters and Congregations, lesser or larger; nor did ever the

working

working *Masons* desire their noble and eminent Brothers to get it repeal'd, but always laugh'd at it, for they ever had, and ever will have their own Wages, while they coalesce in due Form, and carefully preserve the Cement under their own *Grand Master*, let *Cowans* do as they please.

Nay, even during this King's Minority, there was a good *Lodge*, under *Grand Master Chicheley*, held at *Canterbury*, as appears from the *Latin* Register of *William Molart* \* Prior of *Canterbury*, in Manuscript, Pap. 88, in which are named *Thomas Stapylton* the *Master*, and *John Morris, Custos de la Lodge Lathomorum*, or *Warden* of the *Lodge* of *Masons*, with fifteen *Fellow Crafts*, and three *Enter'd Prentices*, all named there. And a Record in the Reign of *Edward* VI. says, 'The Company of *Masons*, being
' otherwise termed *Free-Masons*, of auntient Staunding
' ing and good Reckoning, by Means of affable and
' kind Meetings dyverse Tymes, and as a loving
' Brotherhood use to do, did frequent this mutual
' Assembly in the Tyme of *Henry* VI, in the twelfth
' Year of his most gracious Reign. viz. A. D. 1434,
' when *Henry* was aged thirteen Years.'

Grand Master *Chicheley* held also a *Lodge* at *Oxford*, where he built *All-Souls-College*, and *Bernard*, now St. *John's College*, &c. till he died 1443, when the King appointed

*William Wanefleet*, Bishop of *Winchester*, to be *Grand Master* in building *Eaton-College* near *Windsor*, and *King's-College, Cambridge*; tho' before the Civil Wars in this Reign, the Chapel of it only was finish'd, a Master-piece of the richest *Gothic* that can hardly be match'd. The King also founded *Christ's-College*,

---

\* Intitled, *Liberatio generalis Domini Gulielmi Prioris Christi Cantuariensis erga festum Natalis Domini* 1429.

*Cambridge*,

*Cambridge* (afterwards finish'd by *Margaret Beaufort* Countess of *Richmond*) and his Queen, *Margaret* of *Anjou*, founded *Queen's-College, Cambridge*, while ingenious *Wanefleet*, at his own Cost, built *Magdalen College, Oxford*, and others about 12 pious Houses.

So that before the King's Troubles the *Masons* were much employ'd, and in great Esteem; for the foresaid Record says farther, " That the Charges, and Laws " of the Free-Masons, have been seen and perused by " our late Sovereign King *Henry* VI, and by the " Lords of his most Honourable Council, who have " allowed them, and declared, that they be right " good, and reasonable to be holden, as they have " been drawn out and collected from the Records of " auntient Tymes."

At last, *Masonry* was neglected during the seventeen Years of the bloody Civil Wars between the two Royal Houses of *Lancaster* and *York*, or the *Red* and *White Roses*: For

*Richard Plantagenet*, Duke of *York*, Son of *Richard* Earl of *Cambridge*, and *Anne Mortimer* the Heiress of *Clarence* (as in the Note Page 92.) claim'd the Crown in Right of his Mother, A. D. 1455, and after 12 sore Battles the *Red Rose* lost the Crown, poor King *Henry* VI was murder'd, and all the Males of every Branch of *Lancaster* were cut off; after *John a Gaunt's* Offspring had reigned 72 Years, A. D. 1471.

*White Rose*, see Page 93.

Thus *Richard* Duke of *York* slain in the Battle of *Wakefield*, 1460.

12. *Edward* IV, crown'd 1461, sometimes a King, and sometimes not a King, till A D. 1471, when *Edward* reign'd without a Rival, and employed the Grand Master *Richard Beauchamp*, Bishop of *Sarum*, to repair the Royal Castles and Palaces after the Wars, and to make the Castle and Chapel of *Windsor* more magnificent;

magnificent, for which the Bishop was made Chancellor of the Garter.

Great Men also repaired and built apace; and now the *Londoners* rebuilt their Walls and Gates; while others rais'd 7 pious Houses. The King died the 9th of *April*, 1483.

13. *Edward* V, a Minor, proclaim'd, but not crown'd. *Richard* Duke of *York*.

These two Sons were said to be murder'd in the *Tower*, by Order of their Uncle and Guardian *Richard* III, on the 23d of *May*, 1483.

*Elizabeth Plantagenet*, Wife of King *Henry* VII.

14. *Richard* III. kill'd and took Possession, and was crowned on the 6th of *July*, 1483, and reigned a wise and valiant Prince, till he was slain bravely contending for the Crown with his Rival *Henry Tewdor*, Earl of *Richmond*, in the Battle of *Bosworth*, *Leicestershire*, on the 22d of *August* 1485, without legal Issue.

So ended the *White Rose*, or House of *York*; and also the 14 Kings call'd *Plantagenets*, of the House of *Anjou*, who had reigned from King *Stephen*'s Death,

A. D. 1154.
During Years 331.
Till A. D. 1485.

For connecting the History.

The Genealogy of the Royal *Tewdors*.

They are clearly descended (tho' not in Male Issue) from *Cadwan* the first King of *Wales*, down to *Roderick Maur*, who partition'd his Kingdom into three Principalities, among his three Sons, and died A. D. 876.

1. *Anarawd*, Prince of *North Wales*, whose Male Issue failed. *Llewelin ap Daffyd*, the last Sovereign Prince of *Wales*, slain in Battle, A. D. 1283, when the *Welsh* began to submit to the Crown of *England*.                                                *Edward*

*Edward* III. King of *England*.

*John a Gaunt* by his third Wife, *Katherine Roet*. See Page 93.

*John Beaufort*, Earl of *Somerset*.

*John Beaufort*, Duke of *Somerset*, after all the Males of *John a Gaunt* were extinct, left his only Child, *viz*. *Margaret Beaufort*.

*Charles* V, King of *France*.

Queen *Katherine*, Widow of King *Henry* V.

2. *Cadelh*, Prince of *South Wales*, whose lineal Male Issue ended in *Gruffyd ap Rhyse*, the last Prince of *South Wales*, who died A. D. 1202. But his Sister, *viz*.

*Gwenlian*, was the Wife of *Ednyfed-Fychan* Lord of *Brynfcingle*.

*Gronw ap Ednyfed*.

*Theodore*, or *Tewdor ap Gronw*.

*Gronw ap Tewdor*.

*Tewdor ap Gronw*, married *Margaret*, Grand-Daughter of *Llewelin ap Daffyd*, the last Sovereign Prince of *Wales*.

*Meredith ap Tewdor*.

*Owen Tewdor*, slain in the Battle of *Mortimer's Cross*, 1461.

*Edmund Tewdor*, Earl of *Richmond*.

*Jasper Tewdor*, Duke of *Bedford*, without Issue.

*Owen Tewdor*, a Monk.

3. *Merfyn*, Prince of *Powis Land*, soon fail'd.

*Henry* VII, *Tewdor*, King of *England*

## CHAP. V.

Masonry *in* England, *from King* Henry VII, *till the* Union *of the Crowns*, A, D. 1603.

WHEN King *Richard* III. was slain at *Bosworth*, his Crown was forthwith put upon the Head of the Conqueror, *Henry Tewdor* Earl of *Richmond*, in the Field of Battle, and the Army proclaim'd him.

1 *Henry* VII, King of *England*, on the 22d of *August* 1485, nor did he ever affect another Title and Claim.

But his *Elizabeth Plantagenet*, Daughter of King *Edward* IV, was truly the Heiress of the Royal *Plantagenets*, and convey'd hereditary Rights to her Offspring.

New Worlds are now discover'd.
The Cape of *Good Hope*, A. D. 1487.
And *America*, A. D. 1493.

In this Reign the *Gothic* Stile was brought to its highest Perfection in *England*, while it had been wholly laid aside in *Italy* by the Revivers of the old *Augustan* Stile, as in Part I. Chap. VII.

*John Islip*, Abbot of *Westminster*, finished the Repairs of that Abbey, A. D. 1493, so as it stood till the late Reparations in our Time.

The Grand Master and Fellows of the Order of St. *John* at *Rhodes* (now *Malta*) assembled at their Grand Lodge, chose King *Henry* their Protector, A. D. 1500.

This Royal *Grand Master* chose for his *Wardens* of *England*, the foresaid *John Islip*, Abbot of *Westminster*, and Sir *Reginald Bray*, Knight of the Garter; or Deputies, by whom the King summoned a *Lodge* of Masters in the Palace, with whom he walked in
ample

ample Form to the East End of *Westminster Abby*, and levelled the Foot-Stone of his famous Chapel, on the 24th of *June*, 1502, tho' it well deserves to stand clean alone, being justly called by our Antiquary *Leland*, the Eighth Wonder of Art, the finest Piece of *Gothic* upon Earth, and the Glory of this Reign. Its Cape-stone was celebrated A. D. 1507.

The King employ'd Grand Warden *Bray* to raise the middle Chapel of *Windsor*, and to rebuild the Palace of *Sheen* upon *Thames*, which the King called *Richmond*; and to enlarge the old Palace of *Greenwich*, calling it *Placentia*, where he built the pretty Box call'd the Queen's House.

He rebuilt *Baynard* Castle, *London*, founded six Monasteries, and turn'd the old Palace of *Savoy* into an Hospital; while others built *Brazen-Nose-College*, *Oxford*, *Jesus* and *St. John's* Colleges, *Cambridge*, and about 8 pious Houses; till the King, aged only 54 Years, died at New *Richmond*, on the 22d of *April* 1509, leaving three Children, viz.

2. *Henry* VIII, *Tewdor*, Prince of *Wales*, aged 18 Years, succeeded his Father, A. D. 1509.

*Margaret Tewdor*, first the Wife of *James* IV, King of *Scotland*, next of *Archibald Dowglass*, Earl of *Angus*, next of *Henry Stewart*, Lord *Methuen*.

*Mary Tewdor*, first Wife of *Lewis* XII, King of *France*; and next of *Charles Brandon*, Duke of *Suffolk*.

Cardinal *Woolsey* was chosen Grand Master, who built *Hampton-Court*, and next rear'd *Whitehall*, the College of *Christ-Church*, *Oxford*, and several more good Edifices, which, upon his Disgrace, were forfeited to the Crown, A. D. 1530.

*Thomas Cromwell*, Earl of *Essex*, was the next Patron of the Craft, under the King; for whom he built St. *James's* Palace, *Christ's Hospital*, *London*, and *Greenwich* Castle. Mean while the King and Parliament threw off the old Yoke of the Pope's Supremacy,

and

and the King was declar'd the supreme Head of the Church, A.D. 1534; and *Wales* was united to *England*, A.D. 1536.

The pious Houses, in Number about 926, were suppress'd, A.D. 1539.

*Cromwell*, Earl of *Essex*, unjustly beheaded, A.D. 1540.

*John Touchet*, Lord *Audley*, became *Grand Master*.

But the Suppression of Religious Houses did not hurt *Masonry*; nay, Architecture of a finer Stile gain'd Ground: For those pious Houses, and their Lands, being sold by the King at easy Rates to the Nobility and Gentry, they built of those Ruins many stately Mansions. Thus Grand Master *Audley* built *Magdalen College, Cambridge*, and his great House of *Audley-End*.

King *Henry* VIII, aged near 56 Years, died on the 28th of *January*, 154⁶⁄₇, and left three Children, *viz.*

3. *Edward* VI, *Tewdor*, born by Queen *Jane Seymour*, a Minor of nine Years, under the Regency of his Mother's Brother, *Edward* Duke of *Somerset*, who establish'd the Protestant Religion; and, as *Grand Master*, built his Palace on the *Strand*, call'd still *Somerset-House*, tho' forfeited to the Crown, A.D. 1552. And when the Regent was beheaded, *John Poynet*, Bishop of *Winchester*, was the Patron of the *Free-Masons*, till the King died without Issue, A.D. 1553.

4. *Mary Tewdor*, Daughter of Queen *Katherine* of *Arragon*, aged 38 Years, succeeded her Brother *Edward* as Queen Sovereign. She restored the *Romish* Religion, and persecuted the *Protestants*; married *Philip* II, King of *Spain*, and died without Issue the 17th of *November*, 1558.

5. *Elizabeth Tewdor*, Daughter of Queen *Ann* of *Bollen*, aged 25 Years, succeeded her Sister *Mary* as Queen Sovereign. She restored the *Protestant* Religion, and was declared supreme Head of the Church. Now learning of all Sorts revived, and the good old
*Augustan*

( 103 )

*Augustan* Stile in *England* began to peep from under its Rubbish, and it would have soon made great Progress, if the Queen had affected Architecture: But hearing the *Masons* had certain Secrets that could not be revealed to her (for that she could not be *Grand Master*) and being jealous of all secret Assemblies, she sent an armed Force to break up their annual *Grand Lodge* at *York*, on St. *John*'s Day, the 27th of *December*, 1561.*

But Sir *Thomas Sackville*, *Grand Master*, took care to make some of the chief Men sent, *Free-Masons*, who then joining in that Community, made an honourable Report to the Queen; and she never more attempted to dislodge or disturb them, but esteemed them as a peculiar Sort of Men that cultivated Peace and Friendship, Arts and Sciences, without meddling in the Affairs of Church or State.

In this Reign some Colleges were built, and many stately Mansions, particularly famous *Burleigh House*: for Travellers had brought home some good Hints of the happy Revival of the *Augustan* Stile in *Italy*, with some of the fine Drawings and Designs of the best Architects, whereby the *English* began apace to slight the *Gothic* Stile, and would have entirely left it off, if the Queen had frankly encouraged the Craft.

Here it is proper to signify the Sentiment and Practice of the old *Masons*, viz. That Kings, and other Male Sovereigns, when made Masons, are *Grand Masters* by Prerogative during Life, and appoint a Deputy, or approve of his Election, to preside over the Fraternity, with the Title and Honours of a *Grand Master*; but if the Sovereign is a Female, or not a Brother, or a Minor under a Regent, tho' a Brother,

―――――――――――――――――――
* This Tradition was firmly believed by all the old *English Masons*.

is negligent of the Craft, then the old Grand Officers may assemble the *Grand Lodge* in due Form to elect a *Grand Master*, tho' not during Life, only he may be annually re-chosen while he and they think fit. *

Accordingly, when Grand Master *Sackville* demitted, A. D. 1567, *Francis Russel*, Earl of *Bedford*, was chosen in the North, and in the South Sir *Thomas Gresham*, who built the first *Royal Exchange* at *London*, A. D. 1570. Next

*Charles Howard*, Earl of *Effingham*, was *Grand Master* in the South till 1588; then *George Hastings*, Earl of *Huntington*, till the Queen died unmarried, on the 24th of *March* 160*. When

The Crowns of *England* and *Scotland* (tho' not yet the Kingdoms) were united in her Successor, viz. *James* VI. *Stewart*, King of *Scotland*, Son of *Mary Stewart* Queen Sovereign, Daughter of King *James* V, Son of King *James* IV, by his Queen *Margaret Tewdor* eldest Daughter of King *Henry* VII. of *England*, by his Queen *Elizabeth Plantagenet* the Heiress of *England*, and he was proclaimed at *London*, *James* I King of *England*, *France*, and *Ireland*, on the 25th of *March* 1603.

---

## CHAP. VI.

### Masonry in Scotland, till the Union of the Crowns.

THE History of the first Kings of the *Scots* in *Albin*, or the western Parts beyond the *Clyde* and the Middle of *Grampian* Hills; and also that of the *Picts* in *Caledonia*, along the *German* Sea Coasts, and towards *England*, not containing much to our

---

* This is the Tradition of the old Masons.

Purpose,

Purpose, we may begin with the Restoration of the Kingdom of *Albin* (according to the *Scottish* Chronicle) made by King *Fergus* II. *Mac Erch*, A.D. 403.

And even after that Period, the History of both these Nations consist mostly of War; only we learn, that the *Picts* were a more mechanical and mercantile People than the *Scots*, had built many Cities, and first founded all the old strong Castles in their Dominion; while the *Scots* affected rather to be a Nation of Soldiers, till

*Kenneth* II. *Mac Alpin*, King of *Scots*, demolish'd the Kingdom of the *Picts*, and so became the first King of all Scotland, A. D. 842. He repair'd the publick Edifices after the Wars, and died A. D. 858. * See his Race below.

But both the Branches of his royal Race were mostly engaged in War, till King *Malcolm* II. *Mac Kenneth*, succeeded his Cousin King *Grimus*, A. D. 1008.

---

\* 1. *Kenneth* II, *Mac Alpin*, died 858.

2. *Donald* V succeeded his Brother *Kenneth* II

3. *Constantin* II, Son of *Kenneth* II, succeeded *Donald* V

4. *Ethus* succeeded *Constantin* II.

5. *Gregory*, Son of King *Congallus* (who had reigned before *Kenneth* II) succeeded *Ethus*, he built *Aberdeen*.

6. *Donald* VI succeeded *Gregory*

7. *Constantin* III succeeded *Donald* VI

8. *Malcolm* I succeeded *Constantin* III, he took *Cumberland* and *Northumberland* from *Edmund* King of *England*, Father of

9. *Indulphus* succeeded *Malcolm* I,

10. *Duffus* who succeeded *Indulphus*

11. *Culenus* succeeded *Duffus*

12. *Kenneth* III succeeded *Culenus*, A. D. 976, the Year after *Edgar* King of *England* died. *Kenneth* enacted the Crown hereditary in his family, and died A. D. 994.

13. *Constantin* IV. succeeded *Kenneth* III *Mogallus* the Prince

14. *Grimus* succeeded *Constantin* IV, and died, A. D. 1008.

15. *Malcolm* II, succeeded *Grimus*, A. D. 1008 *Banclio*, murder'd by *Macbeth*,

For King *Malcolm* II. first compiled the Laws, in the famous Book of *Scotland* call'd *Regiam Majestatem*, partition'd the Land into Baronies, founded the Bishoprick of *Aberdeen* (in Memory of his routing the *Norwegians*, A. D. 1017.) cultivated Arts and Sciences, and fortified his Towns and Castles, till he died, leaving only two Daughters, *viz.*

*Beatrix*, the Eldest, Wife of *Albanach*, *Thane* of the Isles.

*Docha*, the Younger, Wife of *Bethsinleg*, *Thane* of *Angus*

1. *Duncan* I. succeeded his Grandfather, A.D. 1033, murder'd by *Macbeth* 1040, but King *Duncan* I. was the Patriarch of the following Kings in this and the next Page.

2. *Macbeth* kill'd, and took Possession 1040, built the Castles of *Dunsinnan* and *Lumfannan*, &c. and much encouraged the Craft, till cut off by *Macduff*, A. D. 1057.

King *Duncan* I.

3. *Malcolm* III. *Keanmore*, or *Head-great*, was restored when *Macbeth* was slain, 1057. He built the old Church of *Dunfermling*, a royal Sepulchre, and levelled the Foot-stone of the old Cathedral of *Durham*, which he richly endow'd. He fortified his Borders, Castles and Sea-Ports, as the Royal *Grand Master*, and Patron of Arts and Sciences, till he died, A. D. 1093.

4. *Donald Bane*, or *White Donald*, *Malcolm*'s younger Brother mounted the Throne, A. D. 1093, and after the Usurper *Duncan* was slain 1095, *Donald* reigned, till his Nephew, King *Edgar*, imprisoned him for Life, A. D. 1098.

5. *Duncan* II, a Bastard of King *Malcolm*'s, usurp'd, A. D. 1094.

*Malcolm* III, by his Queen *Margaret*, Sister of Prince *Edgar Atheling*, and Grand-daughter of King

*Edmund*

2. *Robert* III, *Stewart*, being sickly, left the Government to the Care of his Brother *Robert* Duke of *Albany*, a great Patron of the Craft, till the King died A. D 1406.

3. *James* I, *Stewart*, tho' unjustly captivated, rul'd by his Regent the said *Robert* Duke of *Albany*

*Henry Wardlow*, Bishop of St. *Andrews*, was now *Grand Master*, and founded the University there, A. D. 1411; tho' it was long before a Place of Education.

*Robert* Duke of *Albany* died A. D. 1420, and his Son Duke *Murdock* was Regent till the King was ransom'd, restor'd, and crown'd, A. D. 1424.

King *James* I, prov'd the best King of *Scotland*, the Patron of the Learned, and countenanc'd the *Lodges* with his Presence, as the Royal *Grand Master*; till he settled an yearly Revenue of 4 Pounds *Scots* (an *English* Noble) to be paid by every Master *Mason* in *Scotland*, to a *Grand Master* chosen by the *Grand Lodge*, and approv'd by the Crown, one nobly born, or an eminent Clergyman who had his Deputies in Cities and Counties *; and every new Brother, at Entrance, paid him also a Fee: His Office impowered him to regulate the Fraternity what should not come under the Cognizance of Law Courts; to him appeal'd both Mason and Lord, or the Builder and Founder, when at variance, in order to prevent Law Pleas; and in

---

2. *Robert* III. *Stewart*, (called *John* formerly) succeeded his Father, A. D. 1390, upon hearing that his only Son *James*, in his Voyage to *France*, was captivated by King *Henry* IV of *England*, tho' in Time of Peace, King *Robert* broke his Heart, 1406.

His second Wife, *Euphemia Ross*, was Queen of *Scotland*.

*Walter Stewart*, Earl of *Athol*, who murder'd King *James* I. at *Perth*.

* This is the Tradition of the old *Scottish* Masons, and found in their Records.

his

his Abſence, they appealed to his Deputy, or Grand Wardens, that reſided next to the Premiſſes.

This Office remain'd till the Civil Wars, A. D. 1640, but is now obſolete; nor can it be reviv'd, but by a Royal *Grand Maſter*. And now the *Maſons* joyfully toaſted, To the KING, and the CRAFT.

This excellent King repaired *Falkland*, and his other Palaces, fortified all his Caſtles and Sea-Ports, and influenc'd the Nobility to follow his Example in much employing the Craft, till he was baſely murder'd in the *Dominicans* Abby at *Perth*, by his Uncle *Walter Stewart*, Earl of *Athol*, A. D. 1437; and being juſtly lamented by all, his Murderers were ſeverely puniſhed.

By his Wife *Joan Beaufort*, eldeſt Daughter of *John Beaufort* Earl of *Somerſet*, eldeſt Son of *John a Gaunt*, by his third Wife *Katherine Roet*, he had

4. *James* II, *Stewart*, a Minor of ſeven Years, under the Regency of Lord *Calendar*.

In this Reign *William Sinclair*, the great Earl of *Orkney* and *Caitneſs*, was *Grand Maſter*, and rebuilt *Roſlin* Chapel near *Edinborough*, a Maſter-piece of the beſt *Gothic*, A. D. 1441. Next, Biſhop *Turnbull* of *Glaſcow*, who founded the Univerſity there, A. D. 1454.

And the King, when of Age, encouraged the Craft till he died, A. D. 1460.

By his Wife *Mary*, Daughter of *Arnold* Duke of *Guelders*,

5. *James* III, *Stewart*, a Minor of ſeven Years, ſucceeded, and when of Age, he employed the Craft in more curious Architecture than any Prince before him, particularly at *Sterling*, where he erected a ſpacious Hall, and a ſplendid Chapel Royal in the Caſtle, by the Direction, firſt of Sir *Robert Cockeran* Grand Maſter, and next of *Alexander* Lord *Forbes*, who continued in Office till the King died, A. D. 1488.

By

*Margaret*, Queen of *Ericus* King of *Norway*.

*Margaret*, the Maiden of *Norway*, died coming over, 1290.

But from the Dissolution of the *Pictish* Kingdom, A, D. 842, the *Gothic* Stile was well improv'd in *Scotland*, during Years 448, till the Maiden of *Norway* died, and the Competition began.

This had been more amply and accurately discovered, if the Learned of *Scotland* had published a *Monasticon Scoticanum*, with an Account of the old Palaces and Castles (as fine as any in *Europe*) before the Competition of *Bruce and Balliol*, in a chronological Deduction: A Work long and much desiderated!

During the Competition, Masonry was neglected; but after the Wars, King *Robert* I, *Bruce*, having settled his Kingdom, forthwith employ'd the Craft in repairing the Castles, Palaces, and pious Houses; and the Nobility and Clergy followed his Example, till he died A. D. 1329.

King *David* II, *Bruce*, after his Restoration, much affected *Masonry*, and built St. *David*'s Tower in *Edinburgh* Castle, till he died without Issue, A. D. 1370, leaving the Crown to his Sister's Son, *viz.*

Royal *Stewart*. See the Note below.

1. *Robert* II, *Stewart*, who left the Care of *Masonry* to the eminent Clergy, then very active in raising fine religious Houses, till he died A. D. 1390.

2. *Robert*

---

### Royal *STEWARTS*

1. *Robert* II, *Stewart*, so called from his hereditary Office that now reverted to the Crown; and hence the King's eldest Son is stiled the Prince and Stewart of *Scotland*. This King was the first Earl of *Strathern*, till his Uncle King *David* died, A. D. 1370, and King *Robert* II. died 1390.

His first Wife, *Elizabeth Muir*, was only Countess of *Strathern*, for she died before he was King. Yet her Son, *viz.*

1. *Robert*

King *Edward* II. of *England* at *Bannockburn*, A. D. 1314, obtained an honourable Peace, and died illustrious, A. D. 1329.

King *David* II *Bruce* succeeded, a Minor of eight Years, born of King Robert's second Wife, was sent to *France* till *Edward Balliol* was expell'd; he was afterwards captivated in *England*, till ransomed, and died without Issue 1370.

*Marjory Bruce*, born of King *Robert's* first Wife *Isabella*, Daughter of *Donald* Earl of *Mar* a Noble *Pict*.

### Descent of the Royal *Stewarts* from *Grimus* King of *Scotland*, who died A. D. 1008.

*Bancho*, *Thane* of *Loch Abyr*, murder'd by *Macbeth*, 1040. See Note, Page 105.

*Fleance* fled to *Wales*, and married *Nerfta*, Daughter of *Gruffyd ap Lewellin*, Prince of *Wales*, and died there.

*Walter* I, the young *Welchman*, came to *Scotland* upon the Restoration of King *Malcolm Keanmore*, who made him heritable Lord High Stewart.

*Alan*, the *Stewart*.

*Alexander* I, the *Stewart*.

*Walter* II, the *Stewart*.

*Alexander* II, the *Stewart*.

*John* the *Stewart*.

Sir *Robert Stewart*, Lord *Darnley*, Patriarch of the *Stewarts* of *Lennox*, from whom descended *Henry* Lord *Darnley*, Father of King *James* VI.

*Walter* III, the *Stewart*, the lineal Male of the old royal Race, and Patriarch of the Royal *Stewarts*, by his Wife *Marjory Bruce*.

King *Robert* II, *Stewart*. See the following Note.

*Alexander* II. rebuilt *Coldingham*, and died A. D. 1249.

*Alexander* III, the last Male from *Duncan* I, died A. D. 1285.

*Margaret*

*Edmund Ironsides*, the *Saxon* Heirefs of *England* (by the *Scots* called St *Margaret*) had

6. *Edgar*, who fucceeded *Donald*, and died without Iffue, 1107.

7. *Alexander* I, fucceeded Brother *Edgar*, built the Abbies of *Dunfermling*, and St. *Colm's Inch*, St. *Michael's* at *Scone*, &c. and pationiz'd the Craft till he died, A. D. 1124, without Iffue.

8 *David* I. fucceeded Brother *Alexander*, built the Abby of *Holyrood-houfe*, and the Cathedrals of four Bifhopricks that he eftablifh'd. The Clergy call'd him St. *David*, for his great Endowments to the Church; and the *Mafons* worfhipped him as their benificent *Grand Mafter*, till he died A. D. 1153.

*Maud*, Wife of *Henry* I. King of *England*
*Maud* the Emprefs.
*Mary*, Wife of *Euftace* Count of *Boulogne*.
*Maud*, Wife of King *Stephen*.

By his Queen *Maude*, the Heirefs of *Huntington*, King *David* I. had *Henry* Prince of *Scotland*, who died before his Father, 1152, leaving three Sons, *viz*.

9 *Malcolm* IV, call'd the Maiden, fucceeded his Grandfather *David*, and died without Iffue, A.D. 1165.

10. *William* the *Lyon* fucceeded Brother *Malcolm*, built a Palace at *Aberdeen*, rebuilt the whole Town of *Perth* after a Fire, and was an excellent *Grand Mafter* by the Affiftance of the Nobility and Clergy, till he died A. D. 1214.

*David*, Earl of *Huntington*, died in *England*, A. D. 1219, but all King *William's* Race failing in the Maiden of *Norway*, the Right of Succeffion was in the Heirs of this *David*; and they made the Competition for the Crown, as in the next Page.

Competition of *Bruce* and *Balliol*.

Prince *David*, Earl of *Huntington*, had three Daughters, *viz.*

1. *Margaret*, Wife of *Alan* Lord *Galloway*
2. *Isabella*, Wife of *Robert Bruce*, an *English* Lord, made Lord of *Anundale* in *Scotland*.
3. *Ada* Wife of Lord *Hastings*.

*Donnegilla*, Wife of *John Balliol*, Lord of *Bernard Castle* in *Durham*.

*John Balliol* the Competitor, as descended from *David*'s eldest Daughter, was declared King of *Scotland*, by the Umpire of the Competition, King *Edward* I. of *England* A. D. 1292, for *John*'s owning him his Superior

But *John* revolting, *Edward* deposed him 1296, banish'd him into *Normandy*, and garrison'd *Scotland* for himself; but the *English* were expell'd, first by Sir *William Wallace*, and next by King *Robert Bruce*.

*Edward Balliol* was by King *Edward* III. of *England* sent to *Scotland*, join'd his Party, expell'd young King *David Bruce*, and was crown'd A. D. 1332, but expell'd 1341. Some say his Race are still in *France*.

*Robert Bruce* the Competitor, as the first Male from Prince *David*; but his Claim was over-ruled by the Umpire, and *Robert* soon died.

*Robert Bruce*, Lord of *Anundale*, and by Marriage Earl of *Carrick*, was by King *Edward* I. made Earl of *Huntington*, to make him easy, and after *John Balliol* was banished, King *Edward* promised to make *Bruce* King of *Scotland*, in order to engage him against *Wallace*, but next Day after the Battle of *Falkirk*, A. D. 1298, at a Conference or Interview, *Wallace* convinc'd *Bruce* of his Error, who never fought more against the *Scots*, and died 1303.

*Robert* I. *Bruce*, fled to *Scotland*, and was crown'd 1306, and after many sore Conflicts, he totally routed
King

2. *Robert* III, *Stewart*, being sickly, left the Government to the Care of his Brother *Robert* Duke of *Albany*, a great Patron of the Craft, till the King died A. D 1406.

3. *James* I, *Stewart*, tho' unjustly captivated, rul'd by his Regent the said *Robert* Duke of *Albany*

*Henry Wardlow*, Bishop of St. *Andrews*, was now *Grand Master*, and founded the University there, A. D. 1411; tho' it was long before a Place of Education.

*Robert* Duke of *Albany* died A. D. 1420, and his Son Duke *Murdock* was Regent till the King was ransom'd, restor'd, and crown'd, A. D. 1424.

King *James* I, prov'd the best King of *Scotland*, the Patron of the Learned, and countenanc'd the *Lodges* with his Presence, as the Royal *Grand Master*; till he settled an yearly Revenue of 4 Pounds *Scots* (an *English* Noble) to be paid by every Master *Mason* in *Scotland*, to a *Grand Master* chosen by the *Grand Lodge*, and approv'd by the Crown, one nobly born, or an eminent Clergyman who had his Deputies in Cities and Counties *; and every new Brother, at Entrance, paid him also a Fee: His Office impowered him to regulate the Fraternity what should not come under the Cognizance of Law Courts; to him appeal'd both Mason and Lord, or the Builder and Founder, when at variance, in order to prevent Law Pleas; and in

---

2. *Robert* III. *Stewart*, (called *John* formerly) succeeded his Father, A. D. 1390, upon hearing that his only Son *James*, in his Voyage to *France*, was captivated by King *Henry* IV of *England*, tho' in Time of Peace, King *Robert* broke his Heart, 1406.

His second Wife, *Euphemia Ross*, was Queen of *Scotland*.

*Walter Stewart*, Earl of *Athol*, who murder'd King *James* I. at *Perth*.

* This is the Tradition of the old *Scottish* Masons, and found in their Records.

his

his Abſence, they appealed to his Deputy, or Grand Wardens, that reſided next to the Premiſſes.

This Office remain'd till the Civil Wars, A. D. 1640, but is now obſolete; nor can it be reviv'd, but by a Royal *Grand Maſter*  And now the *Maſons* joyfully toaſted, To the KING, and the CRAFT.

This excellent King repaired *Falkland*, and his other Palaces, fortified all his Caſtles and Sea-Ports, and influenc'd the Nobility to follow his Example in much employing the Craft, till he was baſely murder'd in the *Dominicans* Abby at *Perth*, by his Uncle *Walter Stewart*, Earl of *Athol*, A. D. 1437; and being juſtly lamented by all, his Murderers were ſeverely puniſhed.

By his Wife *Joan Beaufort*, eldeſt Daughter of *John Beaufort* Earl of *Somerſet*, eldeſt Son of *John a Gaunt*, by his third Wife *Katherine Roet*, he had

4. *James* II, *Stewart*, a Minor of ſeven Years, under the Regency of Lord *Calendar*.

In this Reign *William Sinclair*, the great Earl of *Orkney* and *Caitneſs*, was *Grand Maſter*, and rebuilt *Roſlin* Chapel near *Edinborough*, a Maſter-piece of the beſt *Gothic*, A. D. 1441. Next, Biſhop *Turnbull* of *Glaſcow*, who founded the Univerſity there, A.D. 1454.

And the King, when of Age, encouraged the Craft till he died, A. D. 1460.

By his Wife *Mary*, Daughter of *Arnold* Duke of *Guelders*,

5. *James* III, *Stewart*, a Minor of ſeven Years, ſucceeded, and when of Age, he employed the Craft in more curious Architecture than any Prince before him, particularly at *Sterling*, where he erected a ſpacious Hall, and a ſplendid Chapel Royal in the Caſtle, by the Direction, firſt of Sir *Robert Cockeran* Grand Maſter, and next of *Alexander* Lord *Forbes*, who continued in Office till the King died, A. D. 1488.

By

By his Wife *Margaret*, Daughter of *Chriſtiern* I King of *Denmark*.

6. *James* IV, *Stewart*, aged 16 Years, ſucceeded; and by the Grand Maſter *William Elphinſton*, Biſhop of *Aberdeen*, the King founded the Univerſity there, A. D. 1494. *Elphinſton*, at his own Coſt, founded the curious Bridge of *Dee* near *Aberdeen*, finiſh'd by his Succeſſor Biſhop *Gavin Dunbar*, an excellent Grand Maſter, who built many other fine Structures.

The King delighted moſt in Ship-building, and increaſed his Navy Royal, a very warlike Prince; till aſſiſting the *French* in a Diverſion of War, he was loſt in *Flowden Field*, A. D. 1513.

By his Wife *Margaret Tewdor*, eldeſt Daughter of *Henry* VII. King of *England*, he had

7. *James* V. *Stewart*, a Minor of 17 Months; and, when of Age, he became the ingenious Patron of the Learned, eſpecially of the *Maſons*.

In this Reign the Noble *Gavin Dowglaſs*, Biſhop of *Dunkeld*, was *Grand Maſter* till he died, A. D. 1522. Next,

*George Creighton*, Abbot of *Hollyrood* Houſe, till A. D. 1527;

*Patrick*, Earl of *Lindſay* (the Progenitor of our once *Grand Maſter* the late Earl of *Crawford*) who was ſucceeded in that Office by Sir *David Lindſay*, Lion King at Arms, ſtill mentioned among *Scottiſh* Maſons by the Name of *David Lindſay* the learned Grand Maſter; till the King died, *December* 13, 1542.

By his Wife *Mary*, Daughter of *Claud* of *Lorrain*, Duke of *Guiſe*, he left only

8. *Mary Stewart*, Queen Soveraign of *Scotland*, a Minor of ſeven Days, who became Queen Conſort of *France*; and after the Death of her firſt Huſband King *Francis* II, without Iſſue, ſhe returned to *Scotland*, A. D. 1561, and brought with her ſome fine Connoiſſeurs in the *Auguſtan* Stile.

P

She next married, A. D. 1565, *Henry Stewart*, Lord *Darnley*, eldest Son of *Matthew* Earl of *Lennox*, the lineal Male descended from Sir *Robert Stewart*, Lord *Darnley*, of the old royal Race, as mentioned before.

She fell out with her Nobles, who dethroned her, and being defeated in Battle, she fled for Shelter into *England* 1568, where Queen *Elizabeth* detained her a Prisoner; and at last, for Reasons of State, beheaded her, on the 8th of *Feb* 158$\frac{6}{7}$.

9. *James* VI, *Stewart*, born the 19th of *June* 1566, upon his Mother's Abdication he was crown'd King of *Scotland*, aged 13 Months, under 4 successive Regents; and when aged near 12 Years he assumed the Government, A. D. 1578.

He founded the University of *Edinburgh* A. D. 1580, he sailed to *Denmark*, and married *Ann* Princess Royal, A. D. 1589, when he visited the noble *Tycho Brahe*, the Prince of Astronomers, in his Scarlet Island.

The Nobility and Gentry having divided the Spoil of the Churches Revenues, built many stately Mansions of the Ruins of pious Houses, as was done in *England*; and the Masons began to imitate the *Augustan* Stile, under the Direction of several successive *Grand Masters*.

For after the Death of *David Lindsay*, *Andrew Stewart* Lord *Ochiltree*, was *Grand Master*; next Sir *James Sandilands*, Knight of *Malta*. Then *Claud Hamilton*, Lord *Paisley* (Progenitor of our late Grand Master *Abercorn*) who made King *James* a Brother *Mason*, and continued in Office till the Union of the Crowns, A. D 1603.

Before this Period, not only the Crown was possessed of many fine Palaces and strong Castles, but also the Nobles and Chiefs of Clans had fortified themselves; because of their frequent Feuds or Civil Wars,

and

and the Clergy had built many Abbies, Churches, Monastries, and other pious Houses, of as fine *Gothic* as any in *Europe*, most venerable, sumptuous, and magnificent.

The Fraternity of old met in Monastries in foul Weather, but in fair Weather they met early in the Morning on the Top of Hills, especially on St *John* the Evangelist's Day, and from thence walk'd in due Form to the Place of Dinner, according to the Tradition of the old *Scots* Masons; particularly of those in the ancient Lodges of *Killwinning*, *Sterling*, *Aberdeen*, &c.

---

# PART III.

### *The* HISTORY *of* Masonry *in* IRELAND, *till* Grand Master KINGSTON.

THE antient *Romans* having never invaded *Ireland*, we have no good Vouchers of what happened here before St. *Patrick*, (in the Days of King *Leoghair*, about A. D. 430) He founded St *Patrick*'s at *Aramagh*, and the Priory of St. *Avog* at *Lochderg*, near the Cave call'd St. *Patrick*'s *Purgatory*. But afterwards many pious Houses appear'd throughout *Ireland*.

Nor did the *Anglo-Saxons* invade *Ireland*; but *Bede* and others, in the Eighth Century, affirm, that then many *Britons*, *Saxons*, and *Franks*, resorted to the Schools of *Ireland* for Education.

But the *Norwegians* and *Danes* conquered the most part of the Island; and tho' at first they destroyed the pious Houses, they built many Castles and Forts, with lofty Bacons, to alarm the whole Country in an Hour;

Hour; till they were converted to Christianity by the *Irish*, when the *Danes* built many religious Houses; as at *Dublin*, St. *Mary's-Abby*, and *Christ-Church*, about A. D. 984.

At length *BRIEN BORUM* \* the Grand Monarch of all *Ireland*, of *Heber*'s Race, after defeating the *Danes* in many Battles, totally routed them, A. D. 1039.

So far the greater Part of the *Danes* were forced to sail home, and carried with them the best old Records of *Ireland*, an irreparable Damage! But the Learned of other Nations long to see the remaining Manuscripts of *Ireland* published with good Translations, that, among other Antiquities, the Vestiges of their old *Celtic* Architecture might be traced, if possible; for it is thought the *Augustan* Stile had never been there, and that the *Gothic* was only introduced by St. *Patrick*.

After the Expulsion of the *Danes*, the Milesian Kings of *Ireland* ordered the Palaces, Castles, and pious Houses to be repaired, and much employed the Craft, down to *Roderick O Connor*, the last Monarch of all *Ireland*, who built the wonderful Castle of *Tuam* (now demolished) A. D. 1168.

But the Royal Branches having made themselves petty Sovereigns, were embroiled in frequent Civil Wars: One of them, *viz.*

*Dermot*, King of *Leinster*, being defeated by the others, came to *Henry* II, King of *England*, and got leave to contract with Adventurers, *viz. Richard Stranghow* Earl of *Pembroke*, *Robert Fitz-Stephen* of *Cardigan*, and *Maurice Fitz Gerald*; who brought an

---

\* From whom our worthy Brother the late Earl of *Inchequin*, who was Grand Master in *England* in the Year 1727, is descended in a lineal Male Race.

Army

Army of *Welsh* and *English* to *Dermot*'s Assistance, took in *Dublin*, *Waterford*, and many other Places, which they fortified, and surrendered into the Hands of their King, *Henry* II, as soon as he had followed them into *Ireland*, A. D. 1172.

Kings of *England*, now Lords of *Ireland*.

The *Irish*, not without Reason, say, that King *Henry* II. did not conquer *Ireland*, only some of their petty Kings and Princes, rather than be embroiled in Civil Wars, chose to come under his Protection, and of their own accord received the Laws of *England*, with the Freedom of a Parliament at *Dublin*. But where the *English* chiefly resided, Masonry, and other Arts, were most encouraged.

Thus the said *Strangbow*, Lord Warden of *Ireland*, built the Priory of *Kill-mainham*, A D 1174; while St. *Bar* founded the Abby of *Finbar*.

*John de Courcy*, Earl of *Kingsale*, rebuilt the Abby of St. *Patrick*, in *Down*, A. D. 1183; the Priories of *Nedrum* and St *John*'s, with St. *Mary*'s Abby of *Innys*, &c.

In the Reign of *Richard* I, *Alured*, a Noble *Dane*, built St. *John*'s in *Dublin*; and Arch-bishop *Comin* rebuilt St. *Patrick*'s there, A D. 1190, all of Stone, which before was of Timber and Wattles.

King *John* was King of *Ireland* (as the *Irish* affirm) till his Brother *Richard* died 1199; and afterwards went into *Ireland*, and employed *Henry Launders*, Arch-bishop of *Dublin* and Lord Justice, as Grand Master, in building the Castle of *Dublin*, A. D. 1210, while *William* Earl of *Pembroke* built the Priory of *Kilkenny*.

King *Henry* III, A. D. 1216, granted *Ireland* a Magna Charta, the same with that of *England*. *Felix O Quandam*, Arch-bishop of *Tuam*, rebuilt St. *Mary*'s, *Dublin*, and cover'd it with Lead; while *Hugh de Lacy*,

*Lacy*, Earl of *Ulster*, about A. D. 1230, founded *Corrick-Fergus*, a Friary in *Down*, the Priory of *Ards*, and famous *Trim-Castle*, &c. as Grand Master or Patron of the Craft.

The Native Princes lived pretty well with the *English*, till the Reign of King *Edward* II. when Prince *Edward Bruce* (Brother of *Robert Bruce* King of *Scotland*) headed the Confederate *Irish*, conquer'd the Island, was crown'd King of all *Ireland*, A. D. 1315, and reigned three Years; till Sir *Roger Mortimore*, Earl of *March*, landed with a strong Army, and slew King *Edward Bruce* in Battle.

After this, Masonry in the *English* Settlements revived; and in the North of *Ireland* too, where the *Scots* had gradually settled, and brought with them good *Gothic* Masonry. At last

The Natives regarded the Kings of *England* as the lawful Sovereign Lords of *Ireland*, down to King *Henry* VIII, who, in Defiance of the Pope, proclaimed himself King of *Ireland*, which was confirmed in the Parliament at *Dublin*, A. D. 1542.

Kings of *England*, now Kings of *Ireland*.

*Henry* VIII, King of *Ireland*, was succeeded by his Son King *Edward* VI, and he by his Sister Queen *Mary Tewdor*, who got Pope *Paul* IV. to make her Queen of *Ireland*, succeeded by her Sister Queen *Elizabeth Tewdor*, who founded the famous University of *Dublin*, 1591.

Masonry made a tolerable Progress in *Ireland* in the Reigns of *James* I. and *Charles* I. 'till the Civil Wars, when all the Fabrick was out of Joint, 'till the Restauration, A. D. 1660. after which it was reviv'd by some of the Disciples of *Inigo Jones*, in the Reign of King *Charles* II. who founded the Royal Hospital for old Soldiers, at *Kilmainham* near *Dublin*, with neat and convenient Apartments capable of containing
near

near two thousand Invalids, a spacious and convenient Hall richly adorn'd, a most beautiful Chapel, which easily shews the great Ability and curious Skill of the Architects, a handsome Steeple and Spire; the whole Building carried on and finish'd in the just and true Proportions of the Five Orders. A most magnificent and stately *Tholsel*, or Town-house, in the Center of the City of *Dublin*, and in the Suburbs, the pleasant and delightful Square of *Stephen's-Green*, the largest in *Europe*, being an *English* Mile round, or 1760 Yards.

In the Reign of his Brother, King *James* II, Masonry and Arts were much at a stand by reason of the intestine Broils. But when King *William* III, of ever Glorious and Happy Memory, (to this Kingdom) ascended the Throne, vanquish'd its Enemies, and settled Peace among us, Masonry began again to flourish, and the Arts and Sciences were well cultivated; as may be seen in this and the succeeding Reign, by an excellent Custom-House; a spacious and convenient Barrack for the Garrison, the largest in all *Europe*; a most magnificent and beautiful Library in the University; with many other publick and private Buildings: All under the Direction of *Thomas Burgh*, Esq, Engineer, and Surveyor General of all his Majesty's Forts and Fortifications, &c. in *Ireland*, and a true and faithful Brother.

On his Majesty King *George* I. coming to the Throne, the first of *August*, A. D. 1714, Masonry began to be more conspicuous, and Brethren of the highest Rank openly avowed their Knowledge of the Royal Art, assembled in their several Lodges where they thought most proper and convenient: and, with the greatest Decorum and Exactness, revived and instructed each other in the Mysteries of the Noble Science; still keeping in their View the antient Landmarks,

marks, whereby they avoided every dangerous Rock that might prejudice or dishonour the Craft.

But since his present Majesty King *George* II's Accession to the Throne, on the 11th of *June* 1727, he, with his Royal Sons, *Frederick* Prince of *Wales*, and *William* Duke of *Cumberland*, have proved themselves to be tender, indulgent Fathers to Masons, and glorious Patrons to the Royal Art; generous, benificent and affectionate to Arts and Sciences, beyond the Extent of Wishes, always encouraging Industry, and causing Labour to smile, Joy is apparent in the Face of every Artificer, by reason he reaps the sweet Fruit of his Toil. In his mild and bless'd Reign we see many growing Fabricks raise their lofty Heads throughout the whole Kingdom, and shew to every curious Passenger the true Judgment of the Architects by their just Proportions. Numbers may be mentioned, but I shall confine myself within the Limits of my Author, and his own Words, only mention the Parliament House in *Dublin*, under the Direction of Sir *Edward Lovett Pierce*, more magnificent, and far exceeding that of *Great-Britain*, founded on the 3d of *February* 1728; when the Lord *Carteret*, then Lord-Lieutenant, the Lords Justices, several Peers and Members of Parliament, some eminent Clergy, with many Free-Masons, attended by the King's Yeomen of Guard, and a Detachment of Horse and Foot, made a solemn Procession thither; and the Lord Lieutenant having, in the King's Name levelled the Foot-stone at the South Side, by giving it three Knocks with a Mallet, the Trumpets sounded, the solemn Croud made joyful Acclamations, a Purse of Gold was laid on the Stone for the Masons, who drank, To the KING and the CRAFT, &c. And in the Stone were placed two Silver Medals of King *GEORGE* the Second, and Queen *CAROLINE*,

over

over which a Copper-plate was laid, with the following Inscription.

Serenissimus & Potentissimus
Rex Georgius Secundus
Per Excellent. Dominum
Joannen Dominum & Baron. de Hawnes
Locum Tenentem
Et per Excellent Dominos
Hugonem Archiep. Armachan.
Thomam Windham Cancell.
Guliel. Connolly, Dom Com. Prolocut.
Justiciarios Generales,
Primum Hujusce Domus Parliamen. Lapidem
Posuit,
Tertio Die Februarii MDCCXXVIII.

At last the antient Fraternity of the Free and Accepted Masons in *Ireland*, being assembled in their Grand-Lodge at *Dublin*, chose a Noble Grand Master, in Imitation of their Brethren of *England*, in the third Year of his present Majesty King *George* the Second, A D 1730, even our Noble Brother

*James King*, Lord Viscount *Kingston*, the very next Year after his Lordship had with great Reputation, been the Grand-Master of *England* and he has introduced the same Constitutions and Usages.

Here I beg to take leave of my Author for a while, as he cannot possibly go any farther this Way, and and give you a View of the Succession of Grand-Masters and Grand-Officers in *Ireland* for twenty Years further.

*The Succession of Grand Officers in* Ireland, *from Grand Master* Kingston, *in the Year* 1730, *to Grand Master* Kingsborough, *in the Year* 1750. *Taken from the Records of the Grand Lodge.*

TUESDAY, 6th of *April*, 1731. Grand Lodge in Form. When our Right Worshipful and Noble Brother *James King*, Lord Viscount *Kingston*, was unanimously chosen, and declar'd Grand Master of Masons in *Ireland* for the ensuing Year.

*Wednesday*, 7th of *July*, 1731. Grand Lodge in ample Form. When the Right Worshipful and Right Honourable the Lord *Kingston* was install'd and proclaimed aloud, Grand Master of Masons in *Ireland*, and was most cheerfully congratulated and saluted in the ancient and proper Manner: His Lordship was pleased to appoint *Nicholas Nettirvill*, Lord Viscount *Nettirvill*, his Deputy. The Grand Lodge (as is then antient Practice in *Ireland*) chose the Honourable *William Ponsonby*, and *Dillon Pollard Hampson*, Esqrs, for Grand Wardens, who were all declared, congratulated, and saluted.

*Tuesday* 7th of *December*, 1731. Grand Lodge in ample Form. When the Right Worshipful and Right Honourable the Grand Master took the Chair, attended by his Deputy and the Grand Wardens, the Right Honourable *Thomas* Lord *Southwell*, Sir *Seymour Pile*, Bart. *Henry Plunket*, and *Wentworth Harman*, Esqrs; with many other Brethren of Distinction. The Journal of the House, [and several Rules and Orders for the better Regulation thereof] being read, his Lordship was pleased to signify his Concurrence thereto, by signing them with his Name.

*Tuesday*

*Tuesday* 1st of *February*, 1731. Grand Lodge in Form. Brother *John Pennell* was unanimously chosen and declared Secretary to the Grand Lodge.

The Right Worshipful and Right Honourable the Lord *Kingston*, Grand Master, was pleas'd to acquaint the Grand Lodge, that he appointed his Deputy, the Lord *Nettirvill*, to be his Successor, and accordingly on

*Tuesday* 2d of *May*, 1732. Grand Lodge in Form. The Right Honourable *Nicholas Nettirvill*, Lord Viscount *Nettirvill*, was elected Grand Master of Masons in *Ireland* for the ensuing Year.

His Lordship, on Account of his Health and other necessary Business, could not be in *Dublin* on the proper Time of his Installment; but, by his Letter, appointed *Henry Barnwall*, Lord Viscount *Kingsland*, his Deputy, and the Grand Lodge chose *James Brennan*, M. D. and *Robert Nugent* Esq, Grand Wardens, who were all declared and saluted

*Tuesday* 3d of *October*, 1732. Grand Lodge in due Form. When *George Boyde*, Esq; was chosen Treasurer to the Grand Lodge.

The Right Honourable the Lord *Nettirvill*, Grand Master, was pleas'd to nominate his Deputy, the Lord *Kingsland*, to succeed him as Grand Master, and accordingly on

*Tuesday* 1st of *May*, 1733. Grand Lodge in due Form. The Right Honourable *Henry Barnwall* Lord Viscount *Kingsland*, was elected Grand Master of Masons in *Ireland* for the ensuing Year. And

On *Tuesday* the 14th of *August*. The Grand Lodge assembled in ample Form. When the Right Worshipful and Right Honourable the Lord Viscount *Kingsland* was by Grand Master *Nettirvill*, in the most solemn Manner, installed in *Solomon's* Chair, and proclaimed Grand Master of Masons in *Ireland*. His Lordship was pleas'd to appoint Sir *Marcus Beresford*, Lord Viscount *Tyrone* (then absent) his Deputy;

puty; and *James Brennan* M. D. and Captain *William Cobbe* were chosen Grand Wardens, who were all cheerfully congratulated, and properly saluted.

*Tuesday* 7th of *May*, 1734. Grand Lodge in due Form. When it was order'd, that Application should be made to the Right Worshipful and Right Honourable the Grand Master, to do the Fraternity the great Honour of continuing in his Office another Year; his Lordship kindly agreeing thereto, on

*Monday* the 24th of *June*, Grand Lodge in due Form, he was again proclaim'd Grand Master of Masons for the ensuing Year.

His Lordship was pleased to appoint *James Brennan* M. D. late Senior Grand Warden, to be his Deputy; and *William Cobbe*, and *John Baldwin*, Esqrs; were, by the Grand Lodge, chosen Wardens for the ensuing Year.

His Lordship was pleas'd to nominate *James King*, Lord Viscount *Kingston*, to be his Successor; and at an occasional Lodge held the 10th of *April* 1735, in due Form, his Lordship was again elected Grand Master of Masons in *Ireland* for the ensuing Year; but being then at his Country-house, the Secretary was desired to write to him, and acquaint him therewith: His Lordship in the most polite Manner, return'd his Answer of Condescension, and on *Tuesday* the 24th of *June*, he was proclaimed aloud, Grand Master of Masons, &c with the usual Demonstrations of Joy.

His Lordship then appointed *James Brennan*, M.D. to be his Deputy, and nominated *John Baldwin* and *John Corneille* Esqrs; for Grand Wardens, who were immediately approv'd of, declared, and duly congratulated.

The Right Worshipful, and Right Honourable the Lord *Kingston*, Grand Master, nominated the Right Honourable the Lord Viscount *Tyrone* to be his Successor, who was pleased to signify his Agreement thereto, by

his

his Letter, dated the 12th of *May*; and accordingly, at a stated Meeting of the Grand Lodge, in due Form, on *Tuesday* the 1st of *June* 1736, his Lordship was elected Grand Master of Masons in *Ireland* for the Year ensuing

*Thursday* the 24th of *June* 1736. Grand Lodge in due Form. When the Right Worshipful, and Right Honourable Sir *Marcus Beresford*, Lord Viscount *Tyrone*, was proclaimed Grand Master of Masons with the usual Solemnities.

His Lordship was pleased to appoint *James Brennan*, M. D. to be his Deputy, who, as Proxie, in his Lordship's Name received the usual Honours, Homage, and Congratulations on that Occasion. *John Corneille*, and *William Sandford*, Esqrs, were chosen Grand Wardens, declared, saluted and congratulated as usual.

*July* 6th, 1736. Grand Lodge in Form. When *John Arabin*, Esq; was chosen Treasurer to the Grand Lodge.

The Grand Lodge (by their Secretary's Letter) requested, that his Lordship would do them the great Honour to continue in his Grand Mastership another Year, which his Lordship was pleased to consent to, by a most complaisant, genteel Letter; and on *Friday* the 24th of *June*, 1737, the Right Honourable Sir *Marcus Beresford*, Lord Viscount *Tyrone*, was proclaimed Grand Master of Masons for the second Year; his Lordship being pleased to continue our worthy Brother *James Brennan*, M. D. his Deputy; *Cornelius Callaghan* and *John Putland*, Esqrs; being chosen *Wardens* for the ensuing Year, were declared, and saluted with the usual Ceremonies.

*Tuesday* 27th of *December*, 1737. Grand Lodge in Form. Upon the much lamented Death of our truly worthy Brother Dr. *James Brennan*, the Grand Master was pleased to appoint the Senior Grand Warden

*Cornelius*

*Cornelius Callaghan*, Esq; to be his Deputy; *John Putland* Esq; was elected Senior, and *Kane O' Hara* Esq, Junior Grand Wardens during the Remainder of the Year, and were declared and saluted as such.

*Tuesday* 6th of *June*, 1738. Grand Lodge in due Form. When *William Stewart*, Lord Viscount *Mountjoy*, was elected Grand Master of Masons in *Ireland* for the ensuing Year.

And on *Saturday* the 24th of *June*, 1738. Grand Lodge in ample Form. His Lordship was proclaimed aloud, Grand Master of Masons; who being then present, was, with great Solemnity, installed in *Solomon*'s Chair, and received the unanimous Salutes and Congratulations of the Brethren. His Lordship was pleased to continue *Cornelius Callaghan* Esq; his Deputy, and to nominate *Robert Callaghan* and *Edward Martin*, Esqrs, for Wardens, who were immediately approv'd of, declared, and saluted in Form.

Brother *Thomas Mills*, Gent. was by the Grand Lodge appointed Treasurer.

At an occasional Lodge, in due Form, held on *Wednesday* the 16th of *May*, 1739. The Right Worshipful and Right Honourable the Lord Viscount *Mountjoy* was re-elected Grand Master of Masons in *Ireland* for the ensuing Year, to which his Lordship was pleased to give his Consent, and appoint the same Deputy, *Cornelius Callaghan* Esq; and nominate the same Grand Wardens: But Brother *Robert Callaghan* being willing to decline his Office, the Grand Lodge, at a stated Meeting on *Wednesday* the 6th of *June* 1739, unanimously elected *Edward Martin* Esq; Senior, and *Charles Annesly* Esq; Junior Grand Wardens.

*Monday* 24th of *June* 1739. Grand Lodge in ample Form. When the Right Worshipful, and Right Honourable the Lord Viscount *Mountjoy* was proclaimed aloud, Grand Master of Masons, and immediately installed, with the antient Ceremony, Acclamations

mations and Salutes. The Deputy Grand Master, and Grand Wardens, according to their Degrees, receiv'd the accustom'd Salutes and Congratulations.

*Wednesday* 30th of *January*, 1739. Grand Lodge in ample Form. When *John Baldwin*, Esq; formerly a Grand Warden, was nominated to succeed our late worthy Brother *John Pennell*, as Grand Secretary, by the Right Worshipful and Right Honourable the Grand Master. The Grand Lodge approving of the said Nomination, Brother *John Baldwin* was accordingly declared Grand Secretary, and the Books and Seal committed to his Care.

*Wednesday March* 26, 1740. Grand Lodge in due Form. When *John Baldwin* Esq; Grand Secretary, appointed Brother *Richard Pindar* to be his Deputy.

*Wednesday* 7th of *May*, 1740. Grand Lodge in ample Form. When the Right Worshipful the Grand Master informed the Brethren, that he had directed his Deputy in the Nomination of a Grand Master for the ensuing Year, and immediately his Worship withdrew. The Deputy Grand Master then proposed, the Right Honourable the Lords, *Anglesey, Tullamore,* and *Donneraile*, when the Grand Lodge unanimously elected the Right Honourable *Arthur St. Leger*, Lord Viscount *Donneraile*, Grand Master of Masons in *Ireland* for the ensuing Year.

*Tuesday* 24th of *June*, 1740. Grand Lodge in ample Form. When the Right Worshipful and Right Honourable the Lord Viscount *Donneraile* was proclaimed Grand Master of Masons, and immediately installed in the usual and antient Manner, and receiv'd the Salutes and Congratulations customary on the Occasion.

His Lordship was pleased to appoint *Cornelius Callaghan* Esq; to be his Deputy, and nominated *Edward*

*ward Martin*, and *John Morris*, Esqrs. to be Grand Wardens, who were unanimously approv'd of, declar'd, and properly saluted.

*Wednesday* 3d of *June*, 1741. Grand Lodge in due Form. The Right Worshipful Grand Master (by his Deputy) was pleas'd to nominate the Right Honourable *Charles Moore*, Lord Baron of *Tullamoore*, to succeed him as Grand Master. Accordingly the Grand Lodge elected, and dec'ared, the Right Honourable the Lord *Tullamoore* Grand Master of Masons in *Ireland* for the ensuing Year. And on

*Wednesday* the 24th of *June*, 1741. Grand Lodge in ample Form. The Right Worshipful and Right Honourable the Lord *Tullamoore* was proclaimed aloud, Grand Master of Masons, and was installed properly, in the Presence of our former Grand Master, the Right Honourable the Lord *Mountjoy*, several Brethren of Rank and Distinction, and the Masters and Wardens of Thirty Regular Lodges, who all most cheerfully saluted, and congratulated his Lordship in the Chair.

Who was then pleased to appoint *Cornelius Callaghan* Esq, to be his Deputy, and nominated *Edward Martin* and *John Morris* Esqrs; Grand Wardens, which the Grand Lodge unanimously agreed to, declared, and saluted them properly.

*Wednesday* 5th of *May*, 1742. Grand Lodge in due Form. The Secretary was order'd to write to the Right Worshipful and Right Honourable the Grand Master, to know if his Lordship will do the Fraternity the great Honour of continuing to be their Grand Master another Year; his Lordship was pleased to answer in the Affirmative. And on

*Wednesday* the 2d of *June*, 1742. Grand Lodge in due Form. The Right Worshipful, and Right Honourable the Lord *Tullamoore* was re-elected Grand Master of Masons in *Ireland*, for the ensuing Year.

*Thursday*

*Thursday* the 24th of *June*, 1742. Grand Lodge in due Form. When the Right Worshipful, and Right Honourable the Lord *Tullamoore* was proclaim'd aloud, Grand Master of Masons. His Lordship not being then present, by his Letter, was pleas'd to continue the Right Worshipful *Cornelius Callaghan* Esq; his Deputy, and nominate the former Grand Wardens, *Edward Martin* and *John Morris*, Esqrs; who were confirm'd in their Offices by the Grand Lodge, and cheerfully saluted by all the Brethren present.

*Wednesday* 1st of *December*, 1742. Grand Lodge in due Form. The Worshipful *John Baldwin*, Esq; resign'd the Office of Secretary, which Resignation was accepted of. And on

*Monday* the 27th of *December*, 1742. Grand Lodge in due Form. The Senior Grand Warden recommended Brother *Anthony Rellhan*, Esq, M. D. to the Grand Lodge for Grand Secretary, who was immediately approv'd of, declared, and saluted as such.

The Secretary appointed Brother *Edward Spratt*, then Master of the Lodge No. II. to be his Deputy, who was unanimously approv'd of.

*Wednesay* 1st of *June*, 1743. Grand Lodge in Form. The Right Worshipful the Grand Master was pleased to nominate the Right Honourable Sir *Thomas Southwell*, Lord Baron *Southwell*, to be his Successor, which his Lordship, as a true and faithful Brother, most kindly accepted of, and was unanimously elected, and declared Grand Master of Masons in the Kingdom of *Ireland* for the ensuing Year.

And on *Friday* the 24th of *June*, 1743. Grand Lodge in ample Form. The Right Worshipful, and Right Honourable the Lord *Southwell*, was by Grand Master *Tullamoore* installed in *Solomon*'s Chair, invested with the antient Badges of his Dignity, and proclaimed aloud, Grand Master of Masons.

His Lordship appointed *Cornelius Callaghan* Esq.

his Deputy, and nominated *Edward Martin*, and *Kane Fitzgerald*, Esqrs; for Grand Wardens, who were forthwith approved of, and all declared, and properly saluted.

His Lordship was also pleased to nominate Brother *Edward Spratt* to be Secretary to the Grand Lodge in the Room of Brother *Anthony Rellhan*, Esq; who had resigned, which Nomination was unanimously approv'd of, except by one Member, and Brother *Spratt* declared and saluted as Grand Secretary.

*Wednesday* 5th of *June*, 1744. Grand Lodge in due Form. The Right Worshipful the Grand Master was pleased to nominate *John Allen*, Lord Viscount *Allen*, to be his Successor, who being then out of Town, the Grand Lodge nevertheless elected, and declared him Grand Master of Masons in *Ireland* for the ensuing Year. The Secretary was ordered to write to his Lordship, and acquaint him therewith, which was accordingly done; and he was pleased to return for Answer, That he thanked the Grand Lodge for the Honour they had done him, and would make it his Study to promote their Welfare, their Harmony, and Concord.

*Monday* 15th of *June*, 1744. Grand Lodge in due Form. The Right Worshipful the Grand Master, and the Grand Master Elect, being out of Town, sent their brotherly Affections to the Grand Lodge, by the Deputy Grand Master *Callaghan*, and desired that the Installment of the Grand Master may be deferred a few Days till his Lordship came to Town.

And on *Wednesday* the 4th of *July*, 1744. Grand Lodge in due Form. The Right Worshipful and Right Honourable the Lord Viscount *Allen* was, by the Deputy Grand Master *Callaghan*, installed, invested, and proclaimed Grand Master of Masons; and after receiving the proper Salutes and Congratulations, his Lordship was pleased to continue *Cornelius Callaghan* Esq; Deputy Grand Master, who was forthwith declared and saluted. *Hamilton*

*Hamilton Gorges*, Esq; was nominated Senior Grand Warden, and Mr. *Richard Houghton*, Surgeon, Jun. and tho' neither of them were present, they were unanimously approv'd of, declared, and their Proxies saluted.

His Lordship nominated Brother *Edward Martin*, Esq; late Senior Grand Warden, to be continued Treasurer to the Grand Lodge, which was most cheerfully and unanimously agreed to, and tho' not present was declared such, and his Proxie saluted.

The Secretary received Orders from the Grand Lodge, to wait on Brother *Martin* and acquaint him therewith, and likewise to return him their hearty Thanks for his brotherly Affection to the Craft, and constant Attendance, during the six Years of his Grand Wardenship.

*Wednesday* 15th of *May*, 1745 Grand Lodge most occasionally in Form. When the Right Worshipful and Right Honourable the Lord *Allen* was re-elected, and declared Grand Master of Masons in *Ireland* for the ensuing Year.

*Wednesday* 5th of *June*, Grand Lodge in Form. When we received the melancholy News of the Death of our Right Worshipful Grand Master, which deeply affected the Brotherhood with Sorrow for so sensible a Loss: Several former Grand Masters, and other Noble Brethren, were apply'd to, from time to time, to fill the vacant Chair, but it was declined by all; either on Account of their Business in the Country, or going out of the Kingdom. Then Masonry in *Ireland* might be said to be in a Twilight, for Want of its proper Lustre, till Application was made to the truly Noble, and ever to be esteemed among Masons, the Lord *Kingston*. He, like an affectionate and tender Brother, always ready to espouse the Cause of Truth, Charity, and Virtue, most humanely and readily condescended to illuminate the Cause he had often been a shining Ornament in. And on

*Thursday* 31st of *October*, 1745. Grand Lodge occasionally in Form. The Right Worshipful and Right Honourable *James King*, Lord Viscount *Kingston*, was elected, and declared Grand Master of Masons in *Ireland* for the remaining Part of the Year

His Lordship being then in the Country, was pleased, by his Letter, to let the Grand Lodge know, that he appointed the same Deputy, Brother *Cornelius Callaghan* Esq, to act for him; and nominated the same Wardens, Brother *Hamilton Gorges*, and Brother *Richard Houghton* Esqrs; who were immediately declared, and saluted as usual.

*Wednesday* 7th of *May*, 1746. Grand Lodge in Form. The Right Worshipful, and Right Honourable the Lord *Kingston* was again elected, and declar'd Grand Master of Masons in *Ireland* for the ensuing Year. And on

*Tuesday* the 24th of *June*, 1746. Grand Lodge in Form. The Right Honourable *James King*, Lord Viscount *Kingston*, was, by the Secretary, proclaimed aloud Grand Master of Masons, according to antient Custom.

His Worship being all this Year either in *England*, or at his Country Seat, no Successor was nominated, till

*Wednesday* the 3d of *June*, 1747. Grand Lodge in Form. The Brethren unanimously agreed to appoint Sir *Marmaduke Wyvill*, Bart. Successor, who was immediately elected, and declared Grand Master of Masons in *Ireland* for the Year ensuing.

*Wednesday* 24th of of *June*, 1747. Grand Lodge in ample Form. When the Right Worshipful Sir *Marmaduke Wyvill*, Bart. was proclaimed aloud, Grand Master of Masons, invested with the proper Ensigns and Badges of his Office, and installed in *Solomon*'s Chair. The Brethren, with unanimous Joy, saluted and congratulated him according to ancient Custom.

His

His Worship was pleased to appoint *John Putland*, Esq; formerly one of the Grand Wardens, Deputy Grand Master, who with great Joy was declared and saluted. He also nominated *Boyle Lennox*, Esq; Senior Grand Warden, and *Hans Bailie*, Esq; Junior, who were both unanimously approv'd of, declared, and saluted.

*Wednesday* 8th of *June*, 1748. Grand Lodge in due Form. When the Right Worshipful Sir *Marmaduke Wyvill*, Bart. was re-elected, and declared Grand Master of Masons in *Ireland* for the ensuing Year. And on

*Friday* the 24th of *June*, 1748. Grand Lodge in ample Form. His Worship was proclaimed aloud, Grand Master of Masons, invested, and re-installed; congratulated and saluted, by a numerous assembly of worthy Brethren.

He was pleased to continue our Right Worshipful Brother *Putland* his Deputy, and to nominate the same Grand Wardens as before, who were approv'd of, declared, congratulated, and saluted in proper Form.

*Wednesday* 7th of *June*, 1749. Grand Lodge in ample Form. When the Right Worshipful Sir *Marmaduke Wyvill*, Bart. Grand Master, proposed the Right Honourable Sir *Robert King*, Bart. Lord Baron *Kingsborough*, to be his Successor. The Grand Lodge immediately approved of the Nomination, and elected and declared the Right Honourable the Lord *Kingsborough*, Grand Master of Masons in *Ireland* for the ensuing Year.

His Lordship being then out of Town, the Time of Installment was postponed till he thought proper to name the Day, which was *Wednesday* the 13th of *December*, 1749. Grand Lodge in ample Form; a numerous and polite Assembly of Brethren present. When the Right Worshipful Grand Master *Wyvill*

proclaimed

proclaimed aloud our Noble Brother *Robert King*, Lord Baron *Kingsborough*, Grand Master of Masons; invested him with the proper Badges and Ensigns of his Office, and installed him in *Solomon*'s Chair, with great Solemnity and exact Decorum, and placing himself on his Right-hand made a very eloquent and polite Speech to the Audience proper on the Occasion, who, with unanimous cheerfulness, thanked him for his tender Care and good Government of them during the Time of his Grand Mastership, and then joined in their Homage and Congratulations to his Lordship in the antient, accustomed Manner.

The Grand Master forthwith appointed *John Putland*, Esq; to continue Deputy Grand Master, who was then declared and saluted. *Boyle Lennox*, Esq; was nominated to continue Senior Grand Warden, and the Honourable *Roderick Makenzie*, Esq, to be chosen Junior, who were immediately declared and saluted; Joy and Pleasure then appearing in the Minds and Countenances of all the True and Faithful.

It may be justly said, that within these three last Years Free-Masonry has arrived to the highest Perfection it ever was in *Ireland*, as is observed by many old Brothers who had neglected the Lodges, and lain rusty some Years past, now re-entering among their harmonious Brethren and joining in Concord to strengthen their Cement. Lodges, who were become too numerous for one private Assembly, like the industrious Bees, forming themselves into new Regular Bodies, for more convenient hate, many worthy Brethren, from several Parts of the Kingdom, applying to the Grand Master for his Lordship's Sanction to hold their Communities. One Instance more noble than any other, and more deserving perpetuation, I cannot forbear to mention, which I shall do in the Words of the Transaction, for the Information of those Brethren who have not till now, perhaps, had the Opportunity of knowing it.

*Wednesday*

*Wednesday* 3d of *January*, 1749. Grand Lodge in due Form. The Deputy Grand Master *Putland* acquainted the Grand Lodge, that our late Right Worshipful Grand Master Sir *Marmaduke Wyvill*, Bart. together with the Right Worshipful and Right Honourable the Lord *Kingsborough* our present Grand Master, the Deputy Grand Master and Grand Wardens, and many other Gentlemen of Distinction, have formed themselves into a regular Lodge to consult the Good of the Craft, and, as far as in their Power lies, promote the Welfare of the Fraternity in general.

The Grand Lodge having a thorough Sense of their tender and affectionate Inclinations, immediately came to the following Resolution and Order.

Resolved,

That the Secretary do return the respectful and grateful Thanks of this Grand Lodge to the Noble and Right Worshipful Gentlemen and Brethren, who have so zealously considered, and generously offered their Assistance to the promotion and Honour of the Craft.

Ordered,

That a Registry be opened in the Front of the Grand Register Book for the said Lodge, and that the same shall henceforth be distinguished and known by the Denomination of the *GRAND MASTER's LODGE*; and that all, or any of the Members thereof, who does at any Time think proper to visit the Grand Lodge, shall take place of every other Lodge on the Registry, or Roll Books of this Kingdom; and that each and every of them shall be as fully intituled to all and every of the Privileges and Freedoms thereof, as any other Member or Members that this Grand Lodge is composed of.

*Wednesday* 2d of *May,* 1750 Grand Lodge in Form. When it was unanimously resolv'd, that the Right Worshipful and Right Honourable the Lord *Kingsborough,* our present Grand Master, be, and is, hereby re-elected Grand Master of Masons in *Ireland* for the ensuing Year; not doubting his Lordship's Acceptance thereof, from his known Attachment to the Prosperity and Welfare of the Craft. And on

*Monday* 25th of *June,* the Grand Lodge in Form, his Lordship was proclaim'd Grand Master of Masons as usual; and each of the Grand Officers continued in their Stations, with the accustomed Ceremony and Congratulations.

During this Second Year of his Lordship's Administration, the Almighty Architect, and Grand Master of the whole Creation, probably, was pleased with the Inclination of his Creatures; and from his inexhaustable Flow of Mercy and Goodness, bent the Hearts and Minds of the Brethren on a charitable Project of raising a Fund to build an Edifice, equally capable of containing the Members of the Grand Assembly on their solemn Meetings, as also therein to have musical or other Performances exhibited; and the Emoluments arising therefrom to be distributed among the Indigent, according to their several Necessities. But as that Scheme has been printed, and dispersed among the Lodges, I need say no more of it here: But join, all true and faithful Members of the Fraternity, in Praises and Thanks to that great Author of our *Being,* for all his paternal Kindness, whose all-seeing Eye is ever watchful of our Actions be they ever so secret; whose bountiful Hand is ever ready to aid and assist us in all our Adversities; whose spiritual Grace is ever ready at our Call, to fill our Hearts and Minds with Love and Adoration of him; and whose Strength enables us to practise all the Social Virtues.

## The Old CHARGES of the FREE and ACCEPTED MASONS.

### I CHARGE.

*Concerning God and Religion.*

A Mason is obliged by his Tenure to observe the Moral Law, as a true *Noachida*; and if he rightly understands the Craft, he will never be a stupid Atheist, nor an irreligious Libertine, nor act against Conscience.

In antient Times the Christian Masons were charg'd to comply with the Christian Usages of each Country where they travell'd or work'd. But Masonry being found in all Nations, even of divers Religions, they are now generally charged to adhere to that Religion in which all men agree (leaving each Brother to his own particular Opinion) that is, to be good Men and true, Men of Honour and Honesty, by whatever Names, Religions, or Perswasions, they may be distinguish'd. For they all agree in the three great Articles of *Noah*, enough to preserve the Cement of the Lodge. Thus Masonry is the Centre of their Union, and the happy Means of consiliating Persons that otherwise must have remain'd at a perpetual Distance.

II Charge. *Of the Civil Magistrate, Supreme and Subordinate.*

A Mason must be a peaceable Subject, never to be concerned in Plots against the State, nor disrespectful to inferior Magistrates. Of old, Kings, Princes, and States, encourag'd the Fraternity for their Loyalty, who ever flourish'd most in Times of Peace. But tho'

tho' a Brother is not to be countenanced in his Rebellion against the State, yet if convicted of no other Crime, his Relation to the Lodge remains indefeasible.

### III Charge. *Concerning Lodges.*

A Lodge is a Place where Masons meet to work in. Hence the Assembly, or organized Body of Masons, is called a Lodge; just as the Word Church is expressive both of the Congregation, and of the Place of Worship.

Every Brother should belong to some particular Lodge, and cannot be absent without incurring Censure, if not necessarily detained.

The Men made Masons must be Free-born (or no Bondmen) of mature Age, and of good Report, hail and sound, not deform'd, or dismember'd, at the Time of their making. But no Woman, no Eunuch.

When Men of Quality, Eminence, Wealth, and Learning, apply to be made, they are to be respectfully accepted, after due Examination; for such often prove good Lords (or Founders) of Work, and will not employ *Cowans*, when true Masons can be had; they also make the best Officers of Lodges, and the best Designers, to the Honour and Strength of the Lodge: Nay, from among them, the Fraternity can have a Noble Grand Master. But those Brethren are equally subject to the Charges and Regulations, except in what more immediately concerns operative Masons.

### IV Charge. *Of Masters, Wardens, Fellows, and Prentices.*

All Preferments among Masons is grounded upon real Worth and personal merit only, not upon Seniority. No Master should take a Prentice that is not the Son of honest Parents, a perfect Youth, without

Maim or Defect in his Body, and capable of learning the Mysteries of the Art, that so the Lords (or Founders) may be well served, and the Craft not despised; and that when of Age, and expert, he may become an Enter'd Prentice, or a Free Mason of the lowest Degree, and, upon his Improvements, a Fellow Craft, and a Master Mason, capable to undertake a Lord's Work.

The Wardens are chosen from among the Master Masons, and no Brother can be a Master of a Lodge till he has acted as Warden somewhere, except in extraordinary Cases, or when a Lodge is to be form'd, and none such to be had, for then three Masons, tho' never Masters or Wardens of Lodges before, may be constituted Masters and Wardens of that new Lodge.

But no Number, without three Master Masons, can form a Lodge; and none can be the Grand Master, or a Grand Warden, who has not acted as the Master of a particular Lodge.

V Charge. *Of the Management of the Craft in working.*

All Masons should work hard, and honestly, on working Days, that they may live reputably on Holidays; and the working Hours appointed by Law, or confirmed by Custom, shall be observed.

A Master Mason only must be the Surveyor or Master of Work, who shall undertake the Lord's Work reasonably, shall truly defend his Goods as if they were his own, and shall not give more Wages than just to any Fellow or Prentice.

The Wardens shall be true both to Master and Fellows, taking care of all Things both within and without the Lodge, especially in the Master's Absence; and their Brethren shall obey them.

The Master and the Masons shall faithfully finish the Lord's Work, whether Task or Journey; nor shall take the Work at Task which hath been accustomed to Journey.

None shall shew Envy at a Brother's Prosperity, nor supplant him, or put him out of his Work, if capable to finish it.

All Masons shall meekly receive their Wages without murmuring or Mutiny, and not desert the Master till the Lord's Work is finish'd. They must avoid ill Language, calling each other Brother, or Fellow, with much Courtesy, both within and without the Lodge. They shall instruct a younger Brother to become bright and expert, that the Lord's Materials may not be spoiled.

But Free and Accepted Masons shall not allow *Cowans* to work with them; nor shall they be employed by *Cowans* without an urgent Necessity, and even in that Case they must not teach *Cowans*, but must have a seperate Communication.

No Labourer shall be employed in the proper Work of Free Masons.

VI Charge. *Concerning Masons Behaviour.*

1. Behaviour in the Lodge before closing.

You must not hold private Committees, or seperate Conversation, without Leave from the Master; nor talk of any thing impertinent; nor interrupt the Master or Wardens, or any Brother speaking to the Chair, nor act ludicrously while the Lodge is engaged in what is serious and solemn. But you are to pay due Reverence to the Master, Wardens and Fellows, and put them to Worship.

Every Brother found guilty of a Fault, shall stand to the Award of the Lodge, unless he appeals to the Grand Lodge, or unless a Lord's Work is retarded; for then a particular Reference may be made.

No private Piques, no Quarrels about Nations, Families, Religions or Politics, must be brought within the Doors of the Lodge. For, as Masons, we are of the oldest Catholick Religion above hinted, and of all Nations upon the Square, Level, and Plumb: and, like our Predecessors in all Ages, we are resolv'd against political Disputes, as contrary to the Peace and Welfare of the Lodge.

2. Behaviour after the Lodge is closed, and the Brethren not gone.

You may enjoy yourselves with innocent Mirth, treating one another according to Ability, but avoiding all Excess, not forcing any Brother to eat or drink beyond his own Inclination (according to the old Regulation of King *Ahasuerus* ⁎) nor hindering him from going home when he pleases, for tho' after Lodge Hours you are like other Men, yet the Blame of your Excess may be thrown upon the Fraternity, tho unjustly.

3. Behaviour at Meeting without Strangers, but not in a formed Lodge.

You are to salute one another as you have been or shall be instructed, freely communicating Hints of Knowledge, but without disclosing Secrets, unless to those that have given long Proof of their Taciturnity and Honour; and without derogating from the Respect due to any Brother, were he not a Mason: For tho' all Brothers and Fellows are upon the Level, yet Masonry divests no Man of the Honour that was due to him before he was made a Mason, or that shall become his due afterwards; nay, rather, it adds to his Respect, teaching us to give Honour to whom it is due, especially to a Noble or Eminent Brother, whom we should distinguish from all of his Rank and Station, and serve him readily, according to our Ability.

---

⁎ See Page 24.

4. Behaviour

4. *Behaviour in Presence of Strangers, not Masons.*

You must be cautious in your Words, Carriage and Motions, that so the most penetrating Stranger may not be able to discover what is not proper to be intimated, and the impertinent or ensnaring Questions, or ignorant Discourse of Strangers, must be prudently managed by Free-Masons.

5. *Behaviour at Home, and in your Neighbourhood.*

Masons ought to be moral Men, as above charg'd; consequently good Husbands, good Parents, good Sons, and good Neighbours, not staying too long from home, and avoiding all Excess; yet wise Men too, for certain Reasons known to them.

6. *Behaviour towards a foreign Brother, or Stranger.*

You are cautiously to examine him, as Prudence shall direct you, that you may not be imposed upon by a Pretender, whom you are to reject with Derision, and beware of giving him any Hints; but if you discover him to be true and faithful, you are to respect him as a Brother, and if in want, you are to relieve him, if you can, or else direct him how he may be relieved: You must employ him, if you can, or else recommend him to be employed; but you are not charged to do beyond your Ability.

7. *Behaviour behind a Brother's Back, as well as before his Face.*

Free and Accepted Masons have been ever charg'd, to avoid all Slandering and Back-biting of a true and faithful Brother, or talking disrespectfully of his Person or Performances; and all Malice or unjust Resentment: Nay, you must not suffer any others to reproach an honest Brother, but defend his Character as far as is consistent with Honour, Safety, and Prudence, tho' no farther.

VII Charge.

## VII Charge. *Concerning Law-Suits.*

If a Brother do you Injury, apply first to your own or his Lodge, and if you are not satisfied, you may appeal to the Grand Lodge, but you must never take a legal Course, till the Cause cannot be otherwise decided: For if the Affair is only between Masons, and about Masonry, Law-Suits ought to be prevented by the good Advice of prudent Brethren, who are the best Referees of such Differences.

But if that Reference is either impracticable or unsuccessful, and the Affair must be brought into the Courts of Law or Equity, yet still you must avoid all Wrath, Malice and Rancour in carrying on the Suit, not saying or doing any thing that may hinder either the Continuance, or the Renewal of brotherly Love and Friendship, which is the Glory and Cement of this ancient Fraternity; that we may shew to all the World, the benign Influence of Masonry, as all wise, true and faithful Brothers have done from the Beginning of Time, and will do till Architecture shall be absorb'd in the general Conflagration. Amen! So mote it be!

All these Charges you are to observe, and also those that shall be communicated unto you in a Way that cannot be written.

---

*The ancient Manner of constituting a Lodge.*

A New Lodge, for avoiding many Irregularities, should be solemnly constituted by the Grand Master, with his Deputy and Wardens, or in the Grand Master's Absence, the Deputy acts for his Worship, the Senior Grand Warden as Deputy, the Junior Grand Warden as the Senior, and the present Master of a Lodge, as the Junior.

Or

Or if the Deputy is also absent, the Grand Master may depute either of his Grand Wardens, who can appoint others to act as Grand Officers *pro tempore*.

The Lodge being opened, and the Candidates, or the new Master and Wardens being yet among the Fellow Crafts, the Grand Master shall ask his Deputy, if he has examined them, and finds the Candidate Master well skill'd in the Noble Science, and the Royal Art, and duly instructed in our Misteries, &c.

The Deputy answering in the Affirmative, shall (by the Grand Master's Order) take the Candidate from among his Fellows, and present him to the Grand Master, saying; " Right Worshipful Grand
" Master, the Brethren here desire to be formed into
" a regular Lodge, and I present my worthy Brother
" *A. B.* to be their Master, whom I know to be of
" good Morals and great Skill, true and trusty, and
" a Lover of the whole Fraternity, wheresoever dis-
" persed over the Face of the Earth."

Then the Grand Master placing the Candidate on his Left-hand, and having asked and obtained the unanimous Consent of the Brethren, shall say; " I
" constitute and form these good Brethren into a
" new, regular Lodge, and appoint you, Brother
" *A. B.* the Master of it, not doubting of your Ca-
" pacity and Care to preserve the Cement of the
" Lodge, &c" With some other Expressions that are proper and usual on that Occasion, but not proper to be written.

Upon this, the Deputy (or some Brother for him) shall rehearse the Charges of a Master; and the Grand Master shall ask the Candidate, saying, " Do you
" submit to these Charges, as Masters have done in
" all Ages?" And the new Master signifying his cordial Submission thereunto,

The

The Grand Master shall, by certain significant Ceremonies and ancient Usages, install him, and present him with (his Warrant) the Book of Constitutions, the Lodge-book, and the Instruments of his Office, one after another; and after each of them, the Grand Master, his Deputy, or some Brother for him, shall rehearse the short and pithy Charge that is suitable to the Thing presented.

Next the Members of this New Lodge, bowing all together to the Grand Master, shall return his Worship their Thanks; and shall immediately do Homage to their new Master, and signify their Promise of Subjection and Obedience to him, by the usual Congratulation.

The Deputy, and Grand Wardens, and any other Brother present, that are not Members of this new Lodge, shall next congratulate the new Master, and he shall return his becoming Acknowledgments, first to the Grand Master, and to the rest in their Order.

Then the Grand Master orders the new Master to enter immediately upon the Exercise of his Office: And calling forth his Wardens, two Fellow Crafts (Master Masons) presents them to the Grand Master for his Approbation, and to the new Lodge for their Consent. Upon which

The Senior, or Junior Grand Warden, or some Brother for him, shall rehearse the Charge of each Warden of a private Lodge, and they signifying their cordial Submission thereto, the new Master shall present them singly with the several Instruments of their Office, and, in due Form, install them in their proper Places, and the Brethren of this new Lodge shall signify their Obedience to these new Wardens, by the usual Congratulations.

The Grand Master then gives all the Brethren joy of their new Master and Wardens, and recommends

T                                    Harmony,

Harmony, hoping their only Contention will be a laudable Emulation in cultivating the Royal Art, and the Social Virtues.

Upon which all the new Lodge bow together, in returning Thanks for the Honour of this Constitution.

The Grand Master also orders the Secretary to register this new Lodge in the Grand Lodge Book, and to notify the same to the other particular Lodges; and after some other antient Customs, and Demonstrations of Joy and Satisfaction, he orders the Grand Warden to close the Lodge.

---

*A Prayer to be said at the Opening of a Lodge, or making of a Brother.*

MOST holy and glorious Lord God, thou Great Architect of Heaven and Earth, who art the Giver of all good Gifts and Graces; and hast promised, that where two or three are gathered together in thy Name, thou wilt be in the Midst of them; in thy Name we assemble and meet together, most humbly beseeching thee to bless us in all our Undertakings, that we may know and serve thee aright, that all our Doings may tend to thy Glory, and the Salvation of our Souls.

And we beseech thee, O Lord God, to bless this our present Undertaking; and grant that this our new Brother may dedicate his Life to thy Service, and be a true and faithful Brother among us: Endue him with a Competency of thy Divine Wisdom, that he may, with the Secrets of Free-Masonry, be able to unfold the Mysteries of Godliness and Christianity.

This we most humbly beg in the Name, and for the Sake, of Jesus Christ our Lord and Saviour. *Amen.*

The

# The General Regulations of the FREE and ACCEPTED MASONS.

*Agreed to, and approv'd of, by a select Committee appointed by the Grand Lodge in the Year 1739, being the second Year of the Grand Mastership of our Right Worshipful, and Right Honourable Brother the Lord Viscount* Mountjoy *(now Earl of* Blessingtown*) and order'd, by the Grand Lodge, to be observed and practised by all the Lodges in* Ireland.

*Now transcribed, from the Book of Constitutions, published in* England, *in the Year 1738, by our Worshipful Brother* James Anderson, *D. D.*

---

## Old Regulations.

I. THE Grand Master, or Deputy, has full Authority and Right, not only to be present, but also to preside in every Lodge, with the Master of the Lodge on his Left-hand; and to order his Grand Wardens to attend him, who are not to act as Wardens of particular Lodges, but in his Presence, and at his Command: For the Grand Master, while in a particular Lodge, may command the Wardens of that Lodge, or any other Master Masons,

## New Regulations.

I.* THAT is only when the Grand Wardens are absent. For the Grand Master cannot deprive them of their Office, without shewing Cause fairly appearing to the Grand Lodge, according to the Old Regulation XVIII. So that if they are present in a particular Lodge with the Grand Master, they must act as Wardens there.

The Grand Lodge, to cure some Irregularities, order'd, That none but the Grand Master, his Deputy and Wardens, (who

## Old Regulations.

sons, to act there as his Wardens *pro tempore*. *

II. The Master of a particular Lodge has the Right and Authority of congregating the Members of his Lodge into a Chapter, upon any Emergency or Occurrence, as well as to appoint the Time and Place of their usual Forming; and in case of Death, or Sickness, or necessary Absence of the Master, the Senior Warden shall act as Master *pro tempore*, if no Brother is present who has been Master of that Lodge before: For the absent Master's Authority reverts to the last Master present, tho' he cannot act till the Senior Warden has congregated the Lodge.

III. The Master of each particular Lodge, or one of the Wardens, or some other Brother by Appointment of the Master, shall keep

## New Regulations.

(who are the only Grand Officers) shall wear their Jewels in Gold pendant to blue Ribbons about their Necks, and white Leather Aprons with blue Silk; which Sort of Aprons may also be worn by former Grand Officers.

II. It was agreed that if a Master of a particular Lodge is deposed, or demits, the Senior Warden shall forthwith fill the Master's Chair till the next Time of choosing; and ever since, in the Master's Absence, he fills the Chair, even tho' a former Master be present.

Masters and Wardens of particular Lodges may line their white Leather Aprons with white Silk, and may hang their Jewels at white Ribbons about their Necks.

III. If a particular Lodge Remove to a new Place for their stated Meeting, the Officers shall immediately signify the same to the Secretary. The

| Old Regulations. | New Regulations. |
|---|---|
| keep a Book containing their By-Laws, the Names of their Members, and a List of all the Lodges in Town, with the usual Times and Places of their forming; and also the Transactions of their own Lodge, that are proper to be written. | The Precedency of Lodges is grounded on the Seniority of their Constitution. |
| IV. No Lodge shall make more than Five new Brothers at one and the same Time, without an urgent Necessity; nor any Man under the Age of twenty-five Years (who must also be his own Master) unless by a Dispensation from the Grand Master. | IV. No Brother shall belong to more than one Lodge within the Bills of Mortality, (tho' he may visit them all) except the Members of a Foreign Lodge.<br>But this Regulation is neglected for several Reasons, and is now obsolete. |
| V. No Man can be accepted a Member of a particular Lodge, without previous Notice one Month before given to the Lodge, in order to make due Enquiry into the Reputation and Capacity of the Candidate, unless by a Dispensation. | V. The Secretary can direct the Petitioners in the Form for a Dispensation, if wanted; but if they know the Candidate, they don't require a Dispensation. |
| VI. But no Man can be entered a Brother in any particular Lodge, or admitted | VI. No Visitor, however skill'd in Masonry, shall be admitted into a Lodge, |

| Old Regulations. | New Regulations. |
|---|---|
| mitted a Member thereof, without the unanimous Consent of all the Members of that Lodge then present when the Candidate is proposed; and when their Consent is formally asked by the Master, they are to give their Consent in their own prudent Way, either virtually, or in Form, but with Unanimity: Nor is this inherent Privilege subject to a Dispensation; because the Members of a particu- | Lodge, unless he is personally known to, or well vouched and recommended by one of that Lodge then present.<br>But it was found inconvenient to insist upon Unanimity in several Cases; and therefore the Grand Masters have allowed the Lodges to admit a Member, if not above three Ballots are against him; tho' some Lodges desire no such Allowance. |

lar Lodge are the best Judges of it; and because, if a turbulent Member should be imposed on them, it might spoil their Harmony, or hinder the Freedom of their Communication, or even break or disperse the Lodge, which ought to be avoided by all True and Faithful.

| | |
|---|---|
| VII. Every new Brother, at his Entry, is decently to cloath the Lodge, that is, all the Brethren present; and to deposite something for the Relief of indigent and decay'd Brethren, as the Candidate shall think fit to be- | VII.ª See this explained in the Account of the Constitution of the General Charity.<br>Only, particular Lodges are not limitted, but may take their own Method for Charity. |

stow, over and above the small Allowance that may be stated in the By-Laws of that particular Lodge, which Charity shall be kept by the Cashier.ª

Also,

( 151 )

Old Regulations.   New Regulations.

Also, the Candidate shall solemnly promise to submit to the Constitutions, and other good Usages, that shall be intimated to him in Time and Place convenient.

VIII. No Sett or Numbe of Brethren shall withdraw or separate themselves from the Lodge in which they were made, or were afterwards admitted Members, unless the Lodge become too numerous, nor even then, without a Dispensation from the Grand Master or Deputy, and when thus separated, they must either immediately join themselves to such other Lodges that they shall like best, (who are willing to receive them) or else obtain the Grand Master's Warrant to join in forming a new Lodge, to be regularly constituted in good Time.

If any Sett or Number of Masons shall take upon themselves to form a Lodge, without the Grand Master's Warrant, the regular Lodges are not to countenance them, nor

VIII. Every Brother concern'd in making Masons clandestinely, shall not be allowed to visit any Lodge till he has made due Submission; even tho' the Brother so made may be allowed.

None who make a stated Lodge without the Grand Master's Warrant, shall be admitted into regular Lodges, till they make due Submission and obtain Grace.

If any Brethren form a Lodge without leave, and shall irregularly make new Brothers, they shall not be admitted into any regular Lodge, no, not as Visiters, till they render a good Reason, or make due Submission.

If any Lodge within the Limits of the City of *Dublin* shall cease to meet regularly, during twelve Months successive, and not keep up to the Rules and

own

## Old Regulations.

own them as fair Brethren duly form'd, nor approve of their Acts and Deeds; but must treat them as Rebels, until they humble themselves, as the Grand Master shall in his Prudence direct, and until he approve of them, by his Warrant signified to the other Lodges, as the Custom is when a new Lodge is to be register'd in the Grand Lodge-Book.

## New Regulations.

and Orders of the Grand Lodge, its Number and Place shall be erased, or discontinued in the Grand Lodge-Books, and if they petition to be inserted, or owned as a regular Lodge, it must lose its former Place and Rank of Precedency, and submit to a new Constitution.

Seeing that some extraneous Brothers have been made lately in a clandestine Manner, that is, in no regular Lodge, nor by any Authority or Dispensation from the Grand Master, and upon small and unworthy Considerations, to the Dishonour of the Craft;

The Grand Lodge decreed, That no Person so made, nor any concern'd in making him, shall be a Grand Officer, nor an Officer of a particular Lodge; nor shall any such partake of the General Charity, if they should come to want it.

IX. But if any Brother so far misbehave himself as to render his Lodge uneasy, he shall be thrice duly admonished by the Master and Wardens in a Lodge formed. And if he will not refrain his Imprudence, nor obediently submit to the Advice of his Brethren,

IX. Whereas several Disputes have arisen about the Removal of Lodges from one House to another, and it has been questioned in whom that Power is vested; it is hereby declared,

That no Lodge shall be removed without the Master's Knowledge; that no Motion

Old Regulations. | New Regulations.
--- | ---
Brethren, he shall be dealt with according to the By-Laws of that particular Lodge, or else in such a Manner as the Grand Lodge shall, in their great Prudence, think fit; for which a new Regulation may be afterwards made. | Motion be made, for removing in the Master's Absence, and that if the Motion be seconded, or thirded, the Master shall order Summons to every individual Member, specifying the Business, and appointing a Day for hearing and determining the Affair, at least ten

Days before: And the Determination shall be made by the Majority, but if he be of the Minority against removing, the Lodge shall not be removed unless the Majority consists of full two Thirds of the Members present.

But if the Master shall refuse to direct such Summons, either of the Wardens may do it, and if the Master neglects to attend on the Day fix'd, the Warden may preside in determining the Affair, in the Manner prescribed; but they shall not, in the Master's Absence, enter upon any other Cause but what is particularly mentioned in the Summons.

And if the Lodge is thus regularly ordered to be removed, the Master, or Warden, shall send Notice thereof to the Secretary of the Grand Lodge, for publishing the same at the next Meeting of the Grand Lodge.

| | |
|---|---|
| X. The Majority of every particular Lodge, when congregated, (not else) shall have the Privilege of giving Instructions | X. Upon a sudden Emergency, the Grand Lodge has allow'd a private Brother to be present, and with Leave ask'd, |

( 154 )

| Old Regulations. | New Regulations. |
|---|---|
| tions to their Master and Wardens before the Meeting of the Grand Chapter, becauſe the ſaid Officers are their Repreſentatives, and are ſuppoſed to ſpeak the Sentiments of their Brethren at the ſaid Grand Lodge. | aſk'd and given, to ſignify his Mind, if it was about what concerned Maſonry. |
| XI. All particular Lodges are to obſerve the ſame Uſages as much as poſſible; in order to which, and alſo for cultivating a good Underſtanding among Free-Maſons, ſome Members of every Lodge ſhall be deputed to viſit the other Lodges as often as ſhall be thought convenient. | XI. The ſame Uſages, for Subſtance, are actually obſerved in every Lodge; which is much owing to viſiting Brothers, who compare the Uſages. |
| XII. The Grand Lodge conſiſts of, and is formed by the Maſters and Wardens of all the particular Lodges upon Record, with the Grand Maſter at their Head, the Deputy on his Left-hand, and the Grand Wardens in their proper Places. Theſe muſt have their Quarterly Communications, or Monthly Meetings and Adjournments, as often as Occaſion requires, | XII. No new Lodge is owned, nor their Officers admitted into the Grand Lodge, unleſs it be regularly conſtituted and regiſter'd. All who have been, or ſhall be, Grand Maſters, ſhall be Members of, and vote in all Grand Lodges. All who have been, or ſhall be Deputy Grand Maſters, ſhall be Members of, and vote in all Grand Lodges. |

| Old Regulations. | New Regulations. |
|---|---|
| quires, in some convenient Place as the Grand Master shall appoint, where none shall be present but its own proper Members, without Leave asked and given; and while such a Stranger (tho' a Brother) stays, he is not allow'd to vote, nor even to speak to any Question without Leave of the Grand Lodge, or unless he is desired to give his Opinion.<br><br>All Matters in the Grand Lodge are to be determined by a Majority of Votes, each Member having one Vote, and the Grand Master two Votes, | All who have been, or shall be, Grand Wardens, shall be Members of, and vote in all Grand Lodges.<br><br>Masters or Wardens, of particular Lodges, shall never attend the Grand Lodge without their Jewels, except upon giving sufficient Reasons.<br><br>If any Officer of a particular Lodge cannot attend, he may send a Brother of that Lodge (that has been an Officer before) with his Jewel and Cloathing to supply his Room, and support the Honour of his Lodge. |

leave any particular Thing to the Determination of the Grand Master for the Sake of Expedition.

| | |
|---|---|
| XIII. At the Grand Lodge Meeting, all Matters that concern the the Fraternity in General; or particular Lodges, or single Brothers, are sedately and maturely to be discoursed of.<br><br>1. Apprentices must be admitted Fellow Crafts, and Masters only here, unless | XIII. What Business cannot be transacted at one Lodge, may be referred to the Committee of Charity, and by them reported to the next Grand Lodge.<br><br>The Master of a Lodge, with his Wardens and a competent Number of the Lodge assembled in due Form, |

## Old Regulations

unless by a Dispensation from the Grand Master

2. Here also all Differences that cannot be made up or accommodated privately, nor by a particular Lodge, are to be seriously consider'd and decided; and if any Brother thinks himself aggrieved by the Decision, he may appeal to the Grand Lodge next ensuing, and leave his Appeal in Writing with the Grand Master, the Deputy, or Grand Wardens.

## New Regulations.

Form, can make Masters and Fellows at Discretion.

It was agreed in the Grand Lodge, that no Petitions and Appeals shall be heard on the annual Grand Lodge, or Feast Day, nor shall any Business be transacted that tends to interrupt the Harmony of the Assembly, but all shall be referr'd to the next Grand Lodge.

3. Hither also all the Officers of particular Lodges shall bring a List of such Members as have been made, or even admitted by them, since the Grand Lodge.

4. There shall be Books kept by the Grand Master or Deputy, or rather by some Brother appointed Secretary of the Grand Lodge; wherein shall be recorded all the Lodges, with the usual Times and Places of their forming, and the Names of all the Members of each Lodge; also all the Affairs of the Grand Lodge, that are proper to be written.

5. The Grand Lodge shall consider of the most prudent and effectual Method of collecting and disposing of what Money shall be lodged with them on Charity, towards the Relief only of any true Brother fallen into Poverty and Decay, but of none else

6. But each particular Lodge may dispose of their own Charity for poor Brothers, according to their own By-Laws, until it be agreed by all the Lodges

(in a new Regulation *) to carry in the Charity collected by them to the Grand Lodge at their quarterly or annual Communication; in order to make a common stock for the more handsome Relief of poor Brethren.

7. They shall appoint a Treasurer, a Brother of good worldly Substance, who shall be a Member of the Grand Lodge by Virtue of his Office, and shall be always present, and have a Power to move to the Grand Lodge any thing that concerns his Office.

8. To him shall be committed all Money rais'd for the general Charity, or for any other Use of the Grand Lodge, which he shall write down in a Book, with the respective Ends and Uses for which the several Sums are intended, and shall expend or disburse the same, by such a certain Order signed, as the Grand Lodge shall hereafter agree to in a new Regulation. But by Virtue of his Office as Treasurer, without any other Qualification, he shall not vote in chusing a new Grand Master and Wardens; tho' in every other Transaction.

9. In like Manner, the Secretary shall be a Member of the Grand Lodge by Virtue of his Office, and shall vote in every thing except in choosing Grand Officers.

10. The Treasurer and Secretary may have each a Clerk or Assistant, if they think fit, who must be a Brother, and a Master Mason; but must never be a Member of the Grand Lodge, nor speak without being allowed or commanded.

11. The Grand Master, or Deputy, have Authority always to command the Treasurer and Secretary to attend him with their Clerks and Books, in order to see how Matters go on, and to know what is expedient to be done upon any Emergency.

---

* See this explain'd in the Regulation for Charity.

( 158 )

Old Regulations.             New Regulations.

12. Another Brother, and Master Mason, should be appointed the Tyler, to look after the Door; but he must be no Member of the Grand Lodge.

13. But these Offices may be farther explain'd by a new Regulation, when the Necessity or Expediency of them may more appear than at present to the Fraternity.

| XIV. If at any Grand Lodge, stated or occasional, monthly or annual, the Grand Master and Deputy should both be absent; then the present Master of a Lodge, that has been longest a Free-Mason, shall take the Chair, and preside as Grand Master *pro tempore*, and shall be vested with all his Honour and Power for the Time being, provided there is no Brother present that has been Grand Master or Deputy formerly; for the last former Grand Master or Deputy in Company takes place, of right, in the Absence of the present Grand Master or Deputy. | XIV. In the first Edition, the Right of the Grand Wardens was omitted in this Regulation; and it has been since found, that the old Lodges never put into the Chair the Master of a particular Lodge, but when there was no Grand Warden in Company, present nor former; and that in such a Case, a Grand Officer always took place of any Master of a Lodge that has not been a Grand Officer. |

Therefore, in Case of the Absence of all Grand Masters and Deputies, the present Senior Grand Warden fills the Chair, and in his Absence the present Junior Grand Warden, and in his Absence the oldest former Grand Warden in Company; and if no former Grand Officer be found, then the oldest Free-Mason who is now the Master of a Lodge.

But

| Old Regulations. | New Regulations. |
|---|---|

But to avoid Disputes, the Grand Master usually gives a particular Commission under his Hand and Seal of Office, counter signed by the Secretary, to the Senior Grand Warden, or in his Absence to the Junior, to act as Deputy Grand Master when the Deputy is not in Town.

XV. In the Grand Lodge none can act as Wardens but the present Grand Wardens, if in Company; and if absent, the Grand Master shall order private Wardens to act as Grand Wardens *pro tempore*; whose Places are to be supply'd by two Fellow Crafts, or Master Masons of the same Lodge, call'd forth to act, or sent thither by the Master thereof; or if by him omitted, the Grand Master, or he that presides, shall call them forth to act; so that the Grand Lodge may be always compleat.

XV. Soon after the first Edition of the Book of Constitutions, the Grand Lodge finding it was always the antient Usage, that the oldest former Grand Wardens supply'd the Places of those of the Year when absent, the Grand Master ever since has order'd them to take place immediately, and act as Grand Wardens *pro tempore*: which they have always done in the Absence of the Grand Wardens for the Year, except when they have waved their Privilege for that Time, to honour some Brother whom they thought more fit for the present Service.

But if no former Grand Wardens are in Company, the Grand Master, or he that presides, calls forth whom he pleases to act grand Wardens *pro tempore*.

XVI. 1. The Grand Wardens, or any others, are first to advise with the

XVI. 1. This was intended for the Ease of the Grand Master, and for the

| Old Regulations | New Regulations. |
|---|---|
| the Deputy about the Affairs of the Lodges of private single Brothers; and are not to apply to the Grand Master without the Knowledge of the Deputy, unless he refuse his Concurrence. | the Honour of the Deputy. |
| 2. In which Case, or in case of any Difference of Sentiment between the Deputy and Grand Wardens, | 2. No such Case has happened in our Time, and all Grand Masters have governed more by Love than Power |
|  | 3. No irregular Applications have been made to the Grand Master in our Time. |

or other Brothers, both Parties are to go to the Grand Master by Consent; who, by Virtue of his great Authority and Power, can easily decide the Controversy, and make up the Difference.

3. The Grand Master should not receive any private Intimations of Business concerning Masons and Masonry, but from his Deputy first, except in such Cases as his Worship can easily judge of, and if the Application to the Grand Master be irregular, his Worship can order the Grand Wardens, or any other so applying, to wait upon the Deputy, who is speedily to prepare the Business, and to lay it orderly before his Worship.

| | |
|---|---|
| XVII. No Grand Master, Deputy Grand Master, Grand Warden, Treasurer, Secretary, or whoever acts for them, or in their Stead, *pro tempore*, can, at the same Time, act as the Master or Warden of a particular Lodge; but as soon as any of them has | XVII. Old Grand Officers are now, some of them, Officers of particular Lodges; but are not thereby deprived of their Privilege in the Grand Lodge to sit and vote there as old Grand Officers; only he deputes one of his particular |

| Old Regulations. | New Regulations. |
|---|---|
| has discharg'd his publick Office, he returns to that Post or Station in his particular Lodge, from which he was called to officiate. | cular Lodge to act *pro tempore*, as the Officer of that Lodge at the Grand Lodge. |
| XVIII. If the Deputy be sick, or necessarily absent, the Grand Master can choose any Brother he pleases, to act as his Deputy *pro tempore*. | XVIII. 1. The Senior Grand Warden now ever supplies the Deputy's Place, the Junior acts as the Senior, the oldest former Grand Warden as the Junior; also the oldest Mason as above. |
| But he that is chosen Deputy at the Installment, and also the Grand Wardens, cannot be discharged, unless the Cause fairly appear to the Grand Lodge: For the Grand Master, if he is uneasy, may call a Grand Lodge on purpose to lay the Cause before them, for their Advice and Concurrence. | 2. This was never done in our Time. See New Regulation I.<br>3. Should this Case ever happen, the Grand Master appoints his Deputy, and the Grand Lodge the other Grand Officers. |

And if the Members of the Grand Lodge cannot reconcile the Grand Master with his Deputy or Wardens, they are to allow the Grand Master to discharge his Deputy or Wardens, and to choose another Deputy immediately; and the same Grand Lodge, in that Case, shall forthwith choose other Grand Wardens, that so Harmony and Peace may be preserved.

XIX. If

| Old Regulations. | New Regulations. |
|---|---|
| XIX. If the Grand Master should abuse his great Power, and render himself unworthy of the Obedience and Submission of the Lodges, he shall be | XIX. The Free-Masons firmly hope that there never will be any Occasion for such a new Regulation. |

treated in a Way and Manner to be agreed upon in a new Regulation: Because, hitherto, the antient Fraternity have had no Occasion for it.

| XX. The Grand Master, with his Deputy, Grand Wardens, and Secretary, shall, at least once, go round and visit all the Lodges about Town during his Mastership. | XX. Or else he shall send his Grand Officers to visit the Lodges. This old and laudable Practice often renders a Deputy neceseffary: When he visits them, the Senior Grand Warden acts as Deputy, the Junior as |

the Senior, as above; or if both, or any of them be absent, the Deputy, or he that presides for him, may appoint whom he pleases in their stead, *pro tempore*.

For when both the Grand Masters are absent, the Senior or the Junior Grand Warden may preside as Deputy in visiting the Lodges, or in the Constitution of a new Lodge; neither of which can be done without, at least, one of the present Grand Officers.

| XXI. If the Grand Master dies during his Mastership, or by Sickness, or by being beyond Sea, or any other Way be render'd incapable of discharging his Office, the Deputy, or in his Absence the | XXI. Upon such a Vacancy, if no former Grand Master, nor former Deputy be found, the present Senior Grand Warden fills the Chair, or in his Absence the Junior, till a new Grand Master is chosen; and |

| Old Regulations. | New Regulations. |
|---|---|
| the Senior Grand Warden, or in his Absence the Junior Grand Warden, or in his Absence any three Masters of Lodges, shall assemble at | and if no present nor former Grand Warden be found, then the oldest Free-Mason who is now the Master of a Lodge. |

the Grand Lodge immediately, in order to advise together upon the Emergency, and to send two of their Number to invite the last Grand Master to resume his Office, which now of Course reverts to him; and if he refuses to act, then the next last, and so backward, but if no former Grand Master be found, the present Deputy shall act as Principal, till a new Grand Master is chosen; or if there be no Deputy, then the oldest Mason, the present Master of a Lodge.

| XXII. The Brethren of all the Lodges in and near the City of *Dublin*, shall meet in some convenient Place on every St. *John*'s Day, and when Business is over they may repair to their Festival Dinners, as they shall think most convenient; | XXII Or any Brethren around the Globe, who are true and faithful, at the Place appointed, till they have built a Place of their own; but none but Members of the Grand Lodge are admitted in the Doors during the Time of Election of Grand Officers. |

and when St. *John*'s Day shall happen to be on *Sunday*, then the publick Meeting shall be the next *Monday*.

The Grand Lodge must meet in some convenient Place, on St. *John* the Evangelist's Day, on every Year; in order to proclaim the new, or Recognize the old Grand Master, Deputy, and Grand Wardens.

| Old Regulations. | New Regulations. |
|---|---|
| XXIII. If the prefent Grand Mafter fhall confent to continue a fecond Year, then one of the Grand Lodge (deputed for that Purpofe) fhall reprefent to all the Brethren his Worfhip's good Government, &c. and turning to him, fhall in the Name of the Grand Lodge, humbly requeft him to do the Fraternity the great Honour (if nobly born, if not, the great Kindnefs) of continuing to be their Grand Mafter for the Year enfuing; and his Worfhip declaring his Confent thereto (in what Manner he thinks proper) the Secretary fhall proclaim him aloud, *Grand Mafter of Mafons*. All the Members of the Grand Lodge fhall falute him in due Form, according to the antient and laudable Cuftom of Free-Mafons. | XXIII. It was agreed, that Application fhould be made to the Grand Mafter, by the Deputy, (or fuch Brother whom the Grand Lodge fhall appoint, in cafe of his Failure) at leaft one Month before St. *John* the Evangelift's Day, in order to enquire, whether his Worfhip will do the Fraternity the great Honour (or Kindnefs) of continuing in his Office a fecond Year, or of nominating his Succeffor: And if his Worfhip fhould, at that Time, happen to be out of Town, or the Perfon whom he fhall think proper to fucceed him; that then the Secretary fhall write to either, or both, concerning the fame, the Copies of which Letters fhall be tranfcribed in the Tranfaction Book of the Grand Lodge, as alfo the Anfwers received. |

XXIV.

| Old Regulations. | New Regulations. |
|---|---|
| XXIV. The present Grand Master shall nominate his Successor for the Year ensuing, who, if unanimously approv'd of by the Grand Lodge, and there present, he shall be proclaim'd, saluted, and | XXIV. This Regulation has always been put in Practice by the Grand Lodge in *Dublin*; for we never had that Misfortune of disapproving the Choice. |

congratulated the new Grand Master, as above hinted, and immediately installed by the last Grand Master, according to Usage: But if that Nomination is not unanimously approv'd, the new Grand Master shall be chosen immediately by Ballot.

| | |
|---|---|
| XXV. 1. The last Grand Master thus continued, or the new Grand Master thus install'd, shall next, as his inherent Right, nominate and appoint his Deputy Grand Master, (either the last, or a new one) who shall be also proclaimed, saluted, and congratulated, in due Form. | XXV. 1. A Deputy was always needful when the Grand Master was nobly born, and this old Regulation has always been practised in our Time. |
| 2. The new Grand Master shall also nominate his new Grand Wardens, and if unanimously approv'd by the Grand Lodge, they shall also be forthwith proclaimed, saluted, and congratulated, in due Form. | 2. This old Regulation has sometimes been found inconvenient; therefore the Grand Lodge reserve to themselves the Election of Grand Wardens; where any Member has a Right to nominate one; and the two Persons who have the Majority of Voices (still preserving due Harmony) are declared duly elected. |

XXVI.

| Old Regulations. | New Regulations. |
|---|---|
| XXVI. That if the Brother whom the present Grand Master shall nominate for his Successor (or whom the Grand Lodge shall chuse by Ballot as above) be out of Town, and has returned his Answer, that he will accept of the Office of Grand Master, he shall be proclaimed as before in old Regulation XXIII, and may be installed by Proxie, which | XXVI. The Proxie must be either the last or a former Grand Master, (as the Duke of *Richmond* was for Lord *Paisly* in *London*) or else a very reputable Brother, as Lord *Southwell* was for the Earl of *Strathmore*, in the same Place; but the new Deputy, and Grand Wardens, are not allowed Proxies, when appointed. |

Proxie must be the present or a former Grand Master, who shall act, and in his Name receive the usual Honours, Homage, and Congratulations.

| XXVII. Every Grand Lodge has an inherent Power and Authority to make new Regulations, or to alter these, for the real Benefit of the antient Fraternity, provided always that the old Land-Marks be carefully preserved, and that such new Regulations and Alterations be proposed and agreed to by the Grand Lodge; and that they be offered to the perusal of all the Brethren in Writing, | XXVII. All the Alterations, or new Regulations above-written, are only for amending or explaining the old Regulations for the Good of Masonry, without breaking in upon the antient Rules of the Fraternity; still preserving the old Land-marks; and were made at several Times, as Occasion offer'd, by the Grand Lodge, who have an inherent Power of amending what may be thought |

| Old Regulations. | New Regulations. |
|---|---|
| ing, whose Approbation and Consent (or the Majority thereof) is absolutely necessary to make the same binding and obligatory; which must therefore after the new Grand Master is installed, be solemnly desired and obtained from the Grand Lodge, as it was for these old Regulations, by a great Number of Brethren. | thought inconvenient, and ample Authority of making new Regulations for the Good of Masonry; which has not been disputed; for the Members of the Grand Lodge are truly the Representatives of all the Fraternity, according to old Regulation X. |

*The End of the Old Regulations.*

A New Regulation of the Ten following Rules was proposed to the Grand Lodge, and by them agreed to, and ordered to be observed.

XXVIII. 1 That no Brothers be admitted into the Grand Lodge but the immediate Members thereof; *viz.* The four present, and all former Grand Officers; the Treasurer and Secretary, the Masters and Wardens of all Regular Lodges; and all the Members of the Grand Master's Lodge that pleases to attend; except a Brother who is a Petitioner, or a Witness in some Case, or one called in by a Motion.

2. That at the Third Stroke of the Grand Master's Hammer (always to be repeated by the *Senior Grand Warden*) there shall be a general Silence; and that he who breaks Silence, without Leave from the Chair, shall be publickly reprimanded.

3. That

3. That, under the same Penalty, every Brother shall take his Seat, and keep strict Silence, whenever the Grand Master, or Deputy, shall think fit to rise from the Chair and call to Order.

4. That, in the Grand Lodge, every Member shall keep in his Seat, and not move about from Place to Place, during the Communication, except the Grand Wardens, as having more immediately the Care of the Grand Lodge.

5. That no Brother is to speak but once to the same Affair, unless to explain himself, or when call'd by the Chair to speak.

6. Every one that speaks shall rise and keep standing, addressing himself to the Chair; nor shall any presume to interrupt him, under the foresaid Penalty, unless the Grand Master find him wandering from the Point in Hand, shall think fit to reduce him to Order; for then the said Speaker shall sit down; but after he has been set right, he may again proceed, if he pleases.

7. If in the Grand Lodge, any Member is twice called to Order, at any one Assembly, for transgressing these Rules, and is guilty of a third Offence of the same Nature, the Chair shall peremptorily command him to quit the Lodge-room for that Night.

8. That whoever shall be so rude as to hiss at a Brother, or at what another says, or has said, he shall be forthwith solemnly excluded the Communication, and declared incapable of ever being a Member of any Grand Lodge for the future, till another time he publickly owns his Fault, and his Grace be granted.

9. No Motion for a new Regulation, or for the Continuance or Alteration of an old one, shall be made, till it be first handed up in Writing to the Chair; and after it has been perused by the Grand Master, at least about ten Minutes, the Thing may be moved
publickly;

publickly, and then it shall be audibly read by the Secretary, and if he be seconded and thirded, it must be immediately committed to the Consideration of the whole Assembly, that their Sense may be fully heard about it; after which the Question shall be put, Pro and Con.

X. The Opinion or Votes of the Members are always to be signified by each holding up one of his Hands: which uplifted Hands the Grand Wardens are to count, unless the Number of Hands be so unequal as to render the Counting them useless; nor should any other Kind of Division be ever admitted among Masons.

*The End of the New Regulations.*

---

*The* REGULATIONS *of the* COMMITTEE *for* CHARITY, *as they have been approved of and practised by the* Grand Lodge *of* IRELAND *since the Time of Grand Master* Mountjoy *in the Year* 1738.

I. THAT the Committee shall be and consist of the Grand Master, the Deputy Grand Master, and Grand Wardens, and all former Grand Officers, the Treasurer and Secretary, with the Master of every Regular Lodge in the City of Dublin, for the Time being.

II. That all Collections, Contributions, and other charitable Sum or Sums of Money of what Nature or Kind foever, that shall at any Time be brought into the Grand Lodge, shall be deposited in the Hands of the Treasurer, who is not to disburse or expend the same, or any Part thereof, on any Account whatever, without an Order from the said Committee, which Order shall be signed by the Secretary, or the Grand Officer or Master then presiding in the Chair.

III. That neither the Secretary, or any other Person whatever, shall give or sign any Order on the Treasurer for any Sum of Money until the same be first approved of by the Majority of the Committee then present, and entered into their Transaction-book, together with the Name or Names of the Person or Persons to whom the same is to be given.

IV. That no anonymous Letter, Petition, or Recommendation, by or from any Person, or on any Account or Pretence whatsoever, be introduced or read to this Committee.

V. That any Person who shall petition the Grand Lodge, or this Committee for Charity, shall be known to be at least one whole Year a contributing Member to the Fund thereof; and that no Petition shall be received or read in this Committee, but what shall be signed with the Names of (at least) three of the Members thereof, and the Merits of the Petitioner be well vouched by them, or some other worthy Brethren who shall have personal Knowledge thereof: And that no Person shall prefer or bring in any Petition to this Committee but one of the Members who signs it, the Petitioner also attending in Person, except in the Cases of Sickness, Lameness, or Imprisonment.

VI. That it shall be the inherent Power of this
Committee

Committee to dispose of the Fund laid in for Charity to charitable Uses and no other, (and that only to such Persons who shall appear by their Petition, as aforesaid to be deserving and in real Want of charitable and brotherly Assistance,) not exceeding the Sum of Five Pounds to any one Person, or otherwise supply them with a Weekly Support, as they shall judge most necessary.

VII. That no Brother who has received Assistance from this Committee of Charity shall petition a second Time, unless some new and well-attested Allegation appear.

VIII. That no Extraneous Brother, that is, not made in a regular Lodge, but made in a clandestine Manner, or only with a View to partake of this Charity, nor any assisting at such irregular Makings shall be qualified to receive any Assistance therefrom.

IX. That this Committee of Charity may resolve itself into a Committee of the Grand Lodge, at any Time when they shall have Business from the Grand Lodge laid before them, or that the Grand Lodge shall refer any Case to them, when they have too much to do in one Night, and that the Report of the said Committee shall be read in the Grand Lodge, and by them be approved of, before the same shall be put in Execution or Practice.

X. That it is the indispensible Right of the Grand Lodge to order the Committee to meet when they shall judge it necessary, who shall then have Power to adjourn themselves from Time to Time, as the Business may require, at any Time between the Monthly Meetings of the Grand Lodge, where all the preceding Business of the Committee shall be read over, in

Order

Order to inform the Grand Lodge of the Charity expended, and to receive their Concurrence in any Matter that may be referred to them.

XI. That when this Committee is ordered to be assembled, and thereto duly summoned, any eleven of them then meeting shall be a Quorum and proceed upon Business; and if any Debate shall happen to arise, the Majority of Votes then present shall be decisive, always allowing the Grand Officer, or he that shall then preside in the Chair, two Voices, if Occasion require.

*F I N I S.*

# A COLLECTION OF SONGS

To be Sung by

*FREE-MASONS.*

In the old book of Constitutions the Master's song was of too great a length to be sung at one time; therefore the Brethren never sing more than the following verse and chorus.

### I. *The* MASTER's *Song.*

THUS mighty Eastern Kings and some
    Of Abram's race, and monarchs good
Of Egypt, Syria, Greece and Rome,
    True architecture understood.
No wonder then if Masons join
    To celebrate those Mason Kings,
With solemn note, and flowing wine,
    Whilst every brother jointly sings.

### CHORUS.

Who can unfold the Royal Art,
    Or shew its secrets in a song?
They're safely kept in Mason's heart,
    And to the ancient Lodge belong!

*To the King and the Craft.*

In the old book this song was too long, therefore the following last verse, and chorus, is thought sufficient.

## II. *The* WARDEN's *Song.*

FROM henceforth ever sing
 The craftsman, and the king,
With poetry, and musick sweet,
Resound their harmony compleat,
And with Geometry in skilful hand
 Due homage pay,
 Without delay,
To great Kingsborough now our Master Grand,
 He rules the free-born sons of art
 By love and friendship, hand and heart.
### CHORUS
 Who can rehearse the praise
 In soft poetick lays,
Or solid Prose, of Masons true,
Whose art transcends the common view?
Their secrets ne'er to strangers yet expos'd
 Reserv'd shall be
 By Masons free,
And only to the antient Lodge disclos'd;
 Because they're kept in Mason's heart
 By brethren of the Royal Art.

To his Royal Highness (our Brother) *Frederic* Prince of *Wales.*

### III. *The Fellow-Crafts Song.*

#### I.
HAIL Masonry! thou craft divine!
  Glory of earth! from heav'n reveal'd!
Which doth with Jewels precious shine,
  From all but Masons eyes conceal'd.
Chorus. Thy praises due who can rehearse,
  In nervous prose, or flowing verse?

#### II.
As men from brutes distinguish'd are,
  A Mason other men excels;
For what's in knowledge choice and rare
  Within his breast securely dwells
Chor. His silent breast, and faithful heart,
  Preserve the secrets of the art,

#### III.
From scorching heat and piercing cold,
  From beasts whose roar the forest rends,
From the assaults of warriors bold,
  The Mason's art mankind defends.
Chor. Be to this art due honours paid
  From which mankind receives such aid.

#### IV.
Ensigns of state that feed our pride,
  Distinctions troublesome and vain,
By Masons true are laid aside;
  Art's free-born sons such toys disdain.
Chor. Innobled by the name they bear,
  Distinguish'd by the badge they wear.

#### V.
Sweet fellowship from envy free,
  Friendly converse of brotherhood,
The Lodge's lasting cement be
  Which has for ages firmly stood.

A 2 Chorus

( 4 )

Chor. A Lodge thus built, for ages paſt
Has laſted, and ſhall ever laſt.

### VI.

Then in our ſongs be juſtice done
To thoſe who have Inrich'd the art,
From Adam to Kingſborough down,
And let each brother bear a part.
Chor. Let noble Maſons healths go round,
Their praiſe in lofty Lodge reſound.

To his Imperial Majeſty (our brother) *Francis*
Emperor of *Germany*.

---

### IV. *The* Enter'd Prentice's *Song*.

### I.

COME let us prepare,
We brothers that are
Aſſembled on merry occaſion;
Let's drink, laugh, and ſing,
Our wine has a ſpring;
Here's a health to an accepted Maſon.
*All charg'd.*

### II.

The world is in pain
Our ſecrets to gain,
And ſtill let them wonder and gaze on
'Till they're brought to light,
They'll ne'er know the right
Word, or ſign, of an accepted Maſon.

### III.

'Tis this, and 'tis that,
They cannot tell what,
Why ſo many great men of the nation
Should aprons put on,
To make themſelves one
With a free and an accepted Maſon.

### IV.

Great kings, dukes and lords,
Have laid by their swords
Our myst'ry to put a good grace on;
And thought themselves fam'd,
To hear themselves nam'd,
With a free and an accepted Mason.

### V.

Antiquity's pride
We have on our side
And it maketh men just in their Station;
There's nought but what's good
To be understood
By a free and an accepted Mason.

### VI.

We're true and sincere,
And just to the fair,
They'll trust us on any occasion;
No mortal can more
The ladies adore,
Than a free and an accepted Mason.

### VII.

Then joyn hand in hand
By each brother firm stand,
Let's be merry and put a bright face on;
What mortal can boast
So noble a toast,
As a free and an accepted Mason?

### CHORUS.

No mortal can boast
So noble a toast,
As a free and an accepted Mason.

Thrice repeated in due form,

To all the worthy Fraternity round the globe.

## V. *The Deputy* Grand Master's *Song.*

N. B. The two last lines of each verse is the chorus.

### I.
ON, on, my dear brethren, pursue your great lecture,
  And refine on the rules of old architecture.
 High honour to Masons the craft daily brings,
 To those brothers of princes, and fellows of kings.

### II.
We've drove the rude Vandals and Goths off the stage,
Reviving the arts of Augustus' fam'd age.
 Vespasian destroy'd the vast temple in vain,
 Since so many now rise in great George's mild reign.

### III.
Of Wren, and of Angelo, mark the great Names,
Immortal they live, as the Tyber and Thames.
 To heav'n and themselves they've such monuments
   rais'd,
 Recorded like saints, and like saints they are prais'd.

### IV.
The five noble Orders, compos'd with such art,
Will amaze the fixt eye, and engage the whole heart;
 Proportion's dumb harmony gracing the whole,
 Gives our work, like the glorious Creation, a soul.

### V.
Then, Master and brethren, preserve your great name,
This Lodge, so majestic, will purchase you fame;
 Rever'd it shall stand till all nature expire,
 And its glories ne're fade till the world is on fire.

### VI.
See, see, behold here, what rewards all our toil,
Enlivens our genius, and bids labour smile;
 To our noble King(b'rough let a bumper be crown'd,
 To all Masons a bumper, so let it go round.

VII. Again,

### 7.

Again, my lov'd brethren, again let it pass,
Our ancient, firm union cements with the glass:
   And all the contention 'mongst Masons shall be,
   Who better can work, or who best can agree.

*To the Right Honourable the Lord* KINGSBOROUGH,
  *Grand Master of* IRELAND.

---

### VI. *The* Grand Warden's *Song*.

LET Masonry be now my theme,
   Throughout the globe to spread its fame,
And eternize each worthy brother's name.
   Your praise shall to the skies resound,
   In lasting happiness abound,
And with sweet union all your noble deeds be crown'd.
                          *Repeat this line.*

#### CHORUS.

  Sing then, my muse, to Masons glory,
   Your names are so rever'd in story,
That all th'admiring world do now adore ye!

### II.

  Let harmony divine inspire
   Your souls with love and gen'rous fire,
To copy well wise Solomon your Sire.
   Knowledge sublime shall fill each heart
   The rules of g'ometry t'impart,
While wisdom, strength and beauty, crown the glo-
  rious art.

#### CHORUS.

  Sing then, my muse, &c.

### III.

Let great Kingsborough's health go round,
In swelling cups all cares be drown'd,
And hearts united 'mongst the craft be found;

May everlasting scenes of Joy
  His peaceful hours of bliss employ,
Which time's all-conquering hand shall ne'er, shall ne'er destroy.

#### CHORUS.
Sing then, my muse, &c.

#### IV.
My brethren thus all cares resign,
  Your hearts let glow with thoughts divine,
And veneration shew to Solomon's shrine.
  Our annual tribute thus we'll pay,
  That late posterity shall say,
We've crown'd with joy this glorious, happy, happy day.

#### CHORUS.
Sing then, my muse, &c.

To all noble Lords. and right worshipful Brethren, that have been *Grand Masters*.

---

### VII, *The* Treasurer's *Song.*

TUNE, *Near some cool Shade.*

#### I.
GRANT me, kind heaven, what I request;
  In Masonry let me be blest;
Direct me to that happy place
Where friendship smiles in every face;
  Where freedom, and sweet innocence,
  Enlarge the mind, and cheer the sense.

#### II.
Where scepter'd reason from her throne
Surveys the Lodge, and makes us one;
And harmony's delightful sway,
For ever sheds ambrosial day:
  Where we blest Eden's pleasures taste,
  Whilst balmy joys are our repast.

III. Our

### III.

Our Lodge the social virtues grace,
And wisdom's rules we fondly trace;
Whole nature open to our view,
Points out the paths we should pursue:
 Let us subsist in lasting peace,
 And may our happiness increase.

### IV.

No prying eye can view us here,
No fool, or knave, disturb our cheer,
Our well-form'd Laws set mankind free,
And give relief to misery
 The poor, oppress'd with woe and grief,
 Gain from our bounteous hands relief

To all well-disposed charitable Masons.

---

### VIII. *The* Secretary's *Song.*

TUNE, *To you fair Ladies now at land.*

### I.

YE Brethren of the ancient Craft,
 Ye fav'rite sons of Fame,
Let bumpers chearfully be quaff'd
 To great Kingsborough's name.
Happy, long happy may he be;
Who loves and honour's Masonry.
 With a fa, la, la, la, la.

### II.

In vain would D'anvers, with his wit
 Our slow resentment raise;
What he, and all mankind have writ,
 But celebrates our praise.

* That those who hang'd Captain *Porteous* at *Edinburgh* were all Free-Masons, because they kept their own secrets. See *Craftsman* 16th of *April*, Number 563.

His wit this only truth imparts,
'That Masons have firm faithful hearts.
 With a fa, &c.
### III.
Ye British fair, for beauty fam'd,
 Your slaves we wish to be;
Let none for Charms like yours be nam'd
 That love not Masonry:
This maxim D'anvers proves full well,
That Masons never kiss and tell.
 With a fa, &c.
### IV.
True Masons! no offences give,
 Let fame your worth declare,
Within your Compass wisely live,
 And act upon the Square:
May peace and friendship e'er abound,
And great Kingsborough's health go round.
 With a fa, &c.

  To the deputy Grand Master of *Ireland*.

---

## IX. SONG. To the foregoing Tune.

### I.
ON you, who Masonry despise,
 This counsel I bestow:
Don't ridicule, if you are wise,
 A Secret you don't know.
Your selves you banter, but not it;
You shew your spleen, but not your Wit.
 With a fa, la, la, la, la.
### II.
Inspiring virtue by our rules,
 And in our selves secure,
We have compassion for those fools
 Who think our acts impure;

We

We know from ignorance proceeds
Such mean opinions of our deeds.
   With a fa, la, &c.

### III.

If union and sincerity
   Have a pretence to please,
We Brothers of Free-masonry
   Lay justly claim to these;
To state disputes we ne'er give birth,
Our motto Friendship is, and Mirth.
   With a fa, la, &c.

### IV.

Some of our rules I will impart,
   But must conceal the rest,
They're safely lodg'd in Mason's heart,
   Within each honest breast,
We love our Country, and our King,
We toast the ladies, laugh and sing.
   With a fa, la, &c.

*To the Grand Wardens of Ireland.*

---

## X. SONG.

### I.

BY Mason's Art th' aspiring domes
   In stately columns shall arise;
All climates are their natives homes,
   Their well-judg'd actions reach the skies:
Heroes and Kings revere their name,
While Poets sing their lasting fame.

### II.

Great, noble, gen'rous, good, and brave,
   Are titles they most justly claim,
Their deeds shall live beyond the grave,
   Which those unborn shall loud proclaim:

Time shall their glorious acts enrol,
While love and friendship charm the soul.

*To the perpetual honour of Free Masons.*

## XI. SONG.

### I.
AS I at Wheeler's Lodge one night,
 Kept Bacchus company;
For Bacchus is a Mason bright,
 And of all Lodges free.

### II.
Said I, great Bacchus is adry,
 Pray give the God some wine:
Jove, in a fury, did reply,
 October's as divine.

### III.
It makes us Mason's more compleat,
 Adds to our fancy wings,
Makes us as happy, and as great,
 As mighty lords and Kings.

*To the Masters and Wardens of all regular Lodges.*

## XII. SONG.

SOME folks have with curious impertinence strove,
From the Free Masons bosoms their secrets to move;
I'll tell why in vain their endeavours must prove
   Which no body can deny.

### II.
Of that happy secret when we are possest,
Our tongues can't explain what is lodg'd in our breast:
For the blessing's so great it can ne'er be express'd.
   Which no body can deny.

III. By

### III.

By friendship's strict ties we Brothers are join'd,
With mirth in each heart, and content in each mind;
And this is a difficult secret to find.
                Which no body can deny.

### IV.

Truth, charity, justice, our principles are,
What one doth possess, the other may share,
All these, in the world, are secrets most rare.
                Which no body can deny.

### V.

But you who would fain our grand secret disclose,
One thing, best conceal'd to the world you disclose
Much folly, in blaming what none of you knows.
                Which no body can deny.

### VI.

While then we are met, the world's wonder and boast,
And all do enjoy what pleases each most,
I'll give you the best and most glorious toast.
                Which no body can deny.

### VII.

Here's a health to the gen'rous, the brave, and the good,
To all those who think, and who act as they shou'd;
In all this the Free Mason's health's understood.
                Which no body can deny.

---

## XIII. SONG.

TUNE. *Oh! Polly, you might I we toy'd, &c.*

### I.

YE people who laugh at Free Masons draw near,
    Attend to my ballad without any sneer,
And if you'll have patience, you soon shall see,
    What a fine Art is Masonry.

                II. There's

### II.

There's none but an Athiest can ever deny,
But that this great Art came first from on high,
   The Almighty God, here Ill prove for to be
   The first great Master of Masonry.

### III.

He took up his compass with masterly hand,
He stretch'd out his Rule, and he measur'd the land,
   He lay'd the foundations of earth and sea,
   By his known rules of Masonry.

### IV.

Our first father Adam, deny it who can,
A Mason was made, as soon as a man;
   And a fig-leaf apron at first wore he,
   In token of love to Masonry.

### V.

The principle law our Lodge does approve,
Is, that we still live in brotherly love;
   Thus Cain was banish'd by Heaven's decree,
   For breaking the rules of Masonry.

### VI.

The Temple that wise king Solomon rais'd,
For beauty, for order, for elegance, prais'd,
   To what did it owe all its elegancy;
   To the just, form'd rules of Masonry.

### VII.

But should I pretend, in this humble verse,
The merits of Free Masons Arts to rehearse,
   Years yet to come, too little wou'd be
   To sing the praises of Masonry.

### VIII.

Then hoping I have not detain'd you too long,
I here shall take leave to finish my song,
   With a health to the Master, and those who are free,
   That live to the Rules of Masonry.

XIV. SONG.

## XIV. SONG.

WE have no idle prating,
    Of either whigg or tory;
      But each agrees
      To live at ease,
    And sing, or tell a story.
Chorus.     Fill to him
      To the brim,
    Let it round the table rowl,
      The Divine
      Tells you wine
    Cheers the body and the soul.

### II.

We're always men of pleasure,
    Dispising pride and party,
      While knaves and fools
      Prescribe us rules,
    We are sincere and hearty.
Cho.     Fill to him, &c.

### III.

If an accepted Mason
Should talk of high or low church,
      We'll set him down
      A shallow crown,
And understand him no church.
Chor.     Fill to him, &c.

### IV.

The world is all in darkness,
    About us they conjecture,
      But little think
      A song, and drink,
Succeeds the Mason's lecture.
Chor.     Fill to him, &c.

V.

Then, landlord, bring a hogshead,
And in the corner place it,
    Till it rebound
    With hollow sound,
Each Mason here will face it.
Chor.    Fill to him, &c.

---

## XV. SONG.

TUNE, *Young Damon once the happy Swain.*

I.

A Mason's daughter, fair and young,
  The pride of all the virgin throng,
    Thus to her lover said:
Tho', Damon, I your flame approve,
Your actions praise, your person love,
    Yet still I'll live a maid.

II.

None shall untie my virgin zone,
But one to whom the Secret's known
    Of fam'd Free Masonry:
In which the great, and good combine
To raise, with generous design,
    Man to felicity.

III.

The Lodge excludes the fop and fool,
The plodding knave, and party tool,
    That liberty wou'd sell:
The noble, faithful, and the brave,
No golden charms can e'er deceive
    In slavery to dwell.

IV.

This said, he bow'd, and went away;
Apply'd, was made, without delay,

Return'd

Return'd to her again.
The fair one granted his request,
Connubial joys their days have blest,
And may they e'er remain.

## XVI. SONG.

I.

A Health to our Sisters let's drink;
  For why shou'd not they
  Be remember'd, I pray,
When of us they so often do think,
When of us they so often do think.

II.

'Tis they give the chiefest delight,
  The wine cheers the mind,
  And Masonry's kind,
These keep us in transport all night.
These keep us in transport all night.

## XVII. SONG.
TUNE, *The merry ton'd Horn*

SING to the honour of those,
  Who baseness and error oppose;
Who from Sages, and Magi of old,
Have got secrets which none can unfold,
  Whilst thro' life's swift carreer,
  With mirth and good cheer,
    We're revelling
    And levelling
  The monarch, till he
Says, our joys far transcend
What on thrones do attend,
And thinks it a glory like us to be free.

C                II. The

The wisest of kings pav'd the way,
And its precepts we keep to this day;
The most glorious of Temples gave Name
To Free-Masons, who still keep the same,
   Tho' no prince did arise
   So great and so wise,
      Yet in falling
      Our calling
   Still bore high applause.
And tho' darkness o'er-run
   The face of the Sun,
We diamond-like blaz'd, to illumine the cause.

## XVIII. SONG.

TUNE, *Near some cool Shade, O let me keep,*

### I.

GRANT me, kind heav'n, what I request,
   In Masonry let me be blest;
Direct me to that happy place
Where friendship smiles in every face;
Where freedom, and sweet innocence,
Enlarge the mind, and clear the sense.

### II.

Where scepter'd reason, from her throne,
Surveys the Lodge and makes us one,
And harmony's delightful sway
For ever sheds ambrosial day;
Where we blest Eden's pleasures taste,
Whilst balmy joys are our repast.

### III.

No prying eye can view us here,
Or fool, or knave, disturb our cheer.
Our well-form'd laws set mankind free,
And give release to misery;

The poor, oppress'd with woe and grief,
Gain from our bounteous hand relief.
#### IV.
Our Lodge the social virtues grace,
And wisdom's rules we fondly trace;
Whole nature open to our view,
Points out the paths we should pursue,
Let us subsist in lasting peace,
And may our happiness increase.

---

## XIX. SONG.

#### I.
HAIL, sacred Art! by Heaven design'd
To cultivate and cheer the mind;
Thy secrets are to all unknown,
But Masons just and true alone.
But Masons just and true alone.
Chorus.    Then let us all their praises sing,
Fellows to peasant, prince or king.
Fellows to peasant, prince or king.

#### II.
From west to east we take our way,
To meet the bright, approaching day,
That we to work may go in time,
And up the sacred ladder climbe.
And up &c.
Chor.    Then let us all &c.

#### III.
Bright rays of glory did inspire
Our Master great, who came from Tyre,
Still sacred hist'ry keeps his name,
Who did the glorious Temple frame.
Who did &c.
Chor.    Then let us all &c.

#### IV.

The noble Art, divinely rear'd,
Uprightly built upon the Square
  Encompass'd by the pow'rs divine,
  Shall stand until the end of time.
  Shall stand &c.
Chor. Then let us all &c.

#### V.

No human eye thy beauties see
But Masons truly just and free,
  Inspir'd by each heav'nly spark,
  Whilst Cowans labour in the dark.
  Whilst Cowans labour in the dark.
Chor. Then let us all &c.

---

### XX. SONG.

#### I.

COME are you prepar'd,
 Your scaffolds well rear'd,
Bring mortar, and temper it purely;
 'Tis all safe, I hope,
 Well brac'd with each rope,
Your ledgers and putlocks securely.

#### II.

Then next your bricks bring,
It is time to begin,
For the sun with its rays is adorning;
 The day's fair and clear,
 No rain you need fear,
'Tis a charming lovely fine morning.

#### III.

Pray where are your tools,
Your line and plum rules,

Each

Each man to his work let him stand boys,
    Work solid and sure,
    Upright and secure,
And your building, be sure, will be strong boys.

### IV.

    Pray make no mistake,
    But true your joints break,
And take care that you follow your leaders;
    Work, rake back, and rueth,
    And make your work smooth,
And be sure that you fill up your headers.

---

## XXI SONG.

TUNE, *On, on, my dear Brethren.*

### I.

THE curious vulgar could never devise,
    What social Free-Masons so highly do prize:
No human conjecture, no study in schools,
Such fruitless attempts are the actions of fools.

### II.

Sublime are our maxims, our plan from above
Old, as the Creation, cemented with love,
    To promote all the virtues adorning man's life,
    Subduing our passions, preventing all strife.

### III.

Pursue, my dear brethren, embrace with great care,
A system adapted our actions to square,
    Whose origin clearly appeareth divine,
    Observe how its precepts to virtue incline.

### IV.

The secrets of nature king Solomon knew,
The names of all trees in the forest that grew;
    Architecture his study, Free-Masons sole guide,
    Thus finish'd his Temple, antiquities pride.

V. True

#### V.

True, ancient Free-Masons our arts did conceal,
Their hearts were sincere, and not prone to reveal.
 ——Here's the widow's son's mem'ry, that mighty
   great sage,
Who skilfully handled plum, level, and gage.

#### VI.

Toast next our Grand Master, of noble repute,
No Brother presuming his laws to dispute;
 No discord, no faction, our Lodge shall divide,
 Here truth, love, and friendship, must always abide.

#### VII.

Cease, cease, ye vain rebels, your country's disgrace,
To ravage, like Vandals, our Arts to deface:
 Learn, learn, to grow loyal, our King to defend,
 And live like Free-Masons, your lives to amend.

---

### XXII. SONG, To the foregoing Tune.

#### I.

WE brethren, Free-Masons; let's mark the great
   name,
Most antient and loyal, recorded by fame;
 In unity met, let us merrily sing,
 The life of a Mason's like that of a King.

#### II.

No discord, no envy, among us shall be,
No confusion of tongues, but let us all agree!
 Not like building of Babel, confound one another,
 But fill up your glasses, and drink to each Brother.

#### III.

A Tower they wanted to lead them to bliss,
I hope there's no Brother but knows what it is;
 Three principle Steps in our Ladder there be,
 A mist'ry to all, but to those that are free.

IV. Let

### IV.

Let the strength of our reason keep the square of our heart,
And virtue adorn ev'ry man in his part;
   The name of a Cowan we'll not ridicule,
   But pity his folly, and count him a fool.

### V.

Let's lead a good life, whilst power we have,
And when that our bodies are laid in the grave,
   We hope with good conscience to heaven to climb,
   And give Peter the pass-word, the token, and sign.

### VI.

Saint Peter he opens, and so we pass in,
To a place that's prepar'd for all those free from sin.
   To that heavenly Lodge which is tyl'd most secure,
   A place that's prepar'd for all those that are pure.

---

## XXIII. SONG.

TUNE, *What tho' they call me Country Lass.*

### I.

WHAT tho' they call us Masons fools,
   We prove by G'ometry, our rules
Surpass the arts they teach in schools,
   They charge us falsely then:
We make it plainly to appear,
By our behaviour ev'ry where,
That when you meet with Masons, there
   You meet with gentlemen.

### II.

'Tis true, we once have charged been
With disobedience to our Queen,
But after monarchs, plain have seen

The secrets she had sought.
We hatch no plots against the state,
Nor 'gainst great men in power prate,
But all that's noble, good, and great,
 Is daily by us taught.

### III.

These noble structures which we see
Rais'd by our fam'd society,
Surprise the world, then shall not we
 give praise to Masonry.
Let those who do dispise the Art
Live in a Cave, or some desart,
To herd with beasts, from men apart,
 For their stupidity.

### VI.

But view those savage nations where
Free-Masonry did ne'er appear,
What strange unpolish'd brutes they are,
 Then think on Masonry;
It makes us courteous men, alway
Generous, honourable, gay?
What other art, the like can say,
 Then health to Masons free

---

## XXIV. SONG.

### I.

GLORIOUS Craft, which fires the Mind
 With sweet harmony and love,
Surely thou wer't first design'd
 Foretaste of the jo... ove.

### III.

Pleasures alway on thee wait,
 Thou reform'd Adam's race,
Strength and beauty ... meet,
 Wisdoms radiant in thy face.

III. Arts

### III.

Arts and virtues now combine,
    Friendship raises cheerful mirth,
All united to refine
    Man from 'is grosser part of earth.

### IV.

Stately Temples now arise,
    And on lofty columns stand;
Mighty domes attempt the skies
    To adorn this happy land.

---

## XXV. SONG.

### I.

LET malicious people censure,
    They're not worth a Mason's answer.
    While we drink and sing,
    With no conscience-sting.
Let their evil genius plague 'em,
And for Mollies, devil take 'em.
    We'll be free and merry,
    Drink port and sherry,
'Till the stars at midnight shine,
And our eyes with them combine
    The dark night to banish,
    Thus we will replenish
    Nature, whilst the glasses
    With the bottle passes·
    Brother Mason free,
    Here's to thee, to thee;
And let it run the table round,
While envy does the Masons foes confound.

## XXVI. SONG.

### I.

COME, come my Brothers dear,
  Now we're assembled here,
Exalt your voices clear
    With harmony;
Here's none shall be admitted in,
Were he a lord, a duke, or king,
He's counted but an empty thing,
    Except he's free.
Chor. Let ev'ry man take glass in hand,
    Drink bumpers to our Master Grand.
    As long as he can sit, or stand
        With decency.

### II.

By our arts we prove
Emblems of truth and love,
Types given from above
    To those that are free.
There's ne'er a king, that fills a throne,
Will ever be asham'd to own
Those secrets to the world unknown,
    But such as we.
Chor. Let ev'ry man take glass in hand, &c.

### III.

Now, ladies, try your arts,
To gain us, men of parts,
Who best can charm your hearts,
    Because we're free.
Then take us, try us, and you'll find,
We're true and loving, just and kind,
And taught to please a lady's mind
    By Masonry.
Chor. Let ev'ry man take glass in hand, &c.

Grand

( 27 )
Grand Chorus.
God bleſs King GEORGE, long may he reign
To curb the pride of foes that's vain,
And with his conq'ring ſword maintain
Free Maſonry.

---

## XXVII. SONG.

### I.
COME follow, follow me,
 Ye jovial Maſons free;
  Come follow all the rules
  That e'er was taught in ſchools,
By Solomon, that Maſon king,
Who honour to the Craft did bring.

### II.
He's juſtly call'd the wiſe,
His fame doth reach the ſkies,
  He ſtood upon the ſquare,
  And did the Temple rear;
With true level, plumb and gage,
He prov'd the wonder of the age.

### III.
The mighty Maſon Lords
Stood firmly to their words,
  They had it in eſteem,
  For which they're juſtly deem'd,
Why ſhould not their example prove
Our preſent Craft to live in love.

### IV.
The Royal Art, and Word,
Is kept upon record,
  With upright hearts, and pure,
  While ſun and moon endure;
Not written, but indented on
The heart of every Free Maſon.

D 2                    V. And

#### V.

And as for Hiram's art
We need not to impart,
   The scripture plainly shews
   From whence his knowledge flows;
His genious was so much refin'd,
His peer he has not left behind.

#### VI.

Then let not any one
Forget the widow's son,
   But toast his memory
   In glasses charg'd full high,
And when our proper time is come,
Like brethren part, and so go home.

---

## XXVIII. SONG.

#### I.

WITH plumb, level, and square, to work let's prepare,
   And join in a sweet harmony;
Let's fill up each glass, and around let it pass
   To all honest men that are free.
   To all honest men that are free.

#### CHORUS.

Then a fig for all those, who are Free Mason's foes,
   Our secrets we'll never impart;
But in Unity we'll always agree,
   And chorus it, prosper our Art.
   And chorus it prosper our Art.

#### II.

When we're properly cloathed, the Master discloses
   The secrets that's lodg'd in his breast;
Thus we stand by the cause, that deserves great applause,
   In which we are happy and blest,
   In which &c.
Chor. Then a fig for all those, &c.

### III.

The Bible's our guide, and by that we'll abide,
    Which shews that our actions are pure;
The Compass and Square, are emblems most rare
    Of justice our cause to insure.
    Of justice &c.
Chor. Then a fig for all those, &c.

### IV.

The Cowan may strive, nay, plot and contrive,
    To find out our great mystery;
The inquisitive wife, may in vain spend her life,
    For still we'll be honest and free.
    For still &c.
Chor. Then a fig for all those, &c.

### V.

True brotherly love, we always approve,
    Which makes us all mortals excel;
If a knave should by chance, to this grandeur advance,
    That villain we'll straitway expel.
    That villain &c.
Chor. Then a fig for all those, &c.

### VI

So our Lodge that's so pure, to the end shall endure,
    In virtue and true secrecy;
Then let's toast a good health, with honour and wealth,
    To attend the blest hands made us free.
    To attend the kind hands made us free.
Chor. Then a fig for all those, &c.

---

## XXIX. SONG.

### 1.

KING Solomon, that wise projecter,
    In Masonry took great delight;
And Hiram, that great Architecture,
    Whose actions ever shall shine bright.

From the heart of a true honest Mason
   There's none can the secret remove;
Our maxims are justice, morality,
   Friendship, and brotherly love.

### II.

We meet like true friends, on the level,
   And lovingly part on the square;
Alike we respect king and beggar,
   Provided they're just and sincere.
We scorn an ungenerous action,
   None can with Free-Masons compare;
We love for to live within compass,
   By rules that are honest and fair.

### III.

We exclude all talkative fellows,
   That will babble and prate past their wit,
They ne'er shall come into our secret,
   For they're neither worthy, nor fit;
But the person that's well recommended,
   And we find them honest and true,
When our Lodge is well tyl'd we'll prepare them,
   And, like Masons, our work we'll pursue.

### IV.

There's some foolish people reject us,
   For which they are highly to blame,
They cannot shew any objection,
   Or reason for doing the same.
The Art's a divine inspiration,
   As all honest men will declare,
So here's to all true-hearted Brothers,
   That live within Compass and Square.

XXX. SONG.

## XXX. SONG. *By Brother R--P--- Esq;*

TUNE, *By Jove I'll be free.*

### I.

OF all institutions to form well the mind
   And make us to every virtue inclin'd,
None can with the Craft of Free-Masons compare,
Nor teach us so truly our actions to square;
  For it was ordain'd, by our Founder's decree,
  That we should be loyal, be loving, and free.
        Be loving, and free, &c.

### II.

We, in harmony, Friendship, and unity meet,
And every Brother most lovingly greet;
And when we see one in distress still impart
Some comfort to cheer and enliven his heart.
  Thus we always live, and for ever agree,
  Resolv'd to be loyal, most loving, and free.
        Most loving, and free, &c.

### III.

By points of good fellowship we still accord,
Observing each Brother's true sign, grip, and word,
Which from our great Architect was handed down,
And ne'er will to any but Masons be known.
  Then here's to our brethren, of ev'ry degree,
  Who always are loyal, are loving, and free.
        Are loving, and free, &c.

### IV.

Thus we interchangeably hold one another,
To let mankind see how we're link'd to each Brother;
No monarch that secret knot can untie,
Nor can prying mortals the reason know why;
  For our hearts, like our hands, still united shall be,
  Still secret, still loyal, still loving and free.
        Still loving and free, &c.

XXXI. SONG

XXXI. SONG. *To the foregoing Tune,*

By Brother *B---d Cl---ke,*

*Magna est Veritas, & prævalebit.*

### I.
TO the science that virtue, and art do maintain,
Let the muse pay her tribute in soft gliding strain,
Those mistic perfections so fond to display,
As far as allow'd to poetical lay.
    Each profession and class of mankind must agree,
    That Masons alone are the men who are free. &c.

### II.
Their origin they, with great honour, can trace,
From the sons of Religion, and singular grace;
Great Hiram, and Solomon, virtue to prove,
Made this the grand secret of friendship and love.
    Each profession and class of mankind must agree,
    That Masons, of all men, are certainly free, &c.

### III.
The smart, and the beau, the coquet and the prude,
The dull, and the comic, the heavy, and rude,
In vain may enquire, then fret and despise,
An art that's still secret 'gainst all they devise;
    Each profession and class of mankind must agree,
    That Masons, tho' secret, are loyal and free, &c.

### V.
Commit it to thousands, of different mind,
And this golden precept you'll certainly find,
Nor interest, nor terror, can make them reveal,
Without just admittance, what they should conceal,
    Each profession and class of mankind must agree,
    That Masons, alone, are both secret and free, &c.

V. Fair

#### V.

Fair virtue and friendship, religion and love,
The motives of this noble science still prove,
'Tis the key, and the lock, of christ'anity's rules,
And not to be trusted to knaves nor to fools.
    Each profession and class of mankind must agree,
    That Accepted Masons are steady and free, &c.

#### VI.

Th' Isr'lites they distinguish'd their friends from their foes
By signs and characters, then say, why should those
Of vice, and unb'lief, be permitted to pry
Into secrets that Masons alone should descry.
    Each profession and class of mankind must agree,
    That Masons, of all men, are secret and free, &c.

#### VII.

The dunce he imagines that science, and art,
Depends on some compact, or magical part;
Thus men are so stupid, to think that the cause
Of our constitution's against divine laws.
    Each profession and class of mankind must agree,
    That Masons are jovial, religious and free, &c.

#### VIII.

Push about the brisk bowl, let 't circl'ing pass,
Let each chosen Brother lay hold on his Glass,
And drink to the heart that will always conceal,
And the tongue that our secrets will never reveal.
    Each profession and class of mankind must agree,
    That the sons of old Hiram are certainly free, &c.

XXXII SONG

## XXXII. SONG. *By Brother* J--- C---

### TUNE, *Rule Britannia &c.*

#### I.

WHEN earth's foundation first was laid,
  By the Almighty Artist's hand,
'Twas then our perfect, our perfect laws were made,
  Establish'd by his strict command.
Hail! mysterious, hail! glorious Masonry,
That makes us ever great and free.

#### II.

As man throughout for shelter sought,
  In vain from place, to place, did roam,
Until from heaven, from heaven he was taught
  To plan, to build, and fix his home.
Hail! mysterious, &c.

#### III.

Hence, illustrious, rose our Art,
  And now in beauteous piles appear,
Which shall to endless, to endless time impart,
  How worthy, and how great we are.
Hail! mysterious, &c.

#### IV.

Nor we, less fam'd for ev'ry tye
  By which the human thought is bound,
Love, truth and friendship, and friendship socially,
  doth join our hearts and hands around.
Hail! mysterious, &c.

#### V.

Our actions still by virtue blest,
  And to our precepts ever true,
The world admiring, admiring shall request
  To learn, and our bright paths pursue.
Hail! mysterious, hail! glorious Masonry,
That makes us great, and good, and free.

XXXIII. SONG.

## XXXIII. SONG.

#### I.

COME, boys, let us more liquor get,
Since jovially we all are met,
Since jovially we all are met,
   Here none will disagree;
Let's drink and sing and all combine,
In songs to praise that Art divine,
In songs to praise that Art divine,
   That's call'd Free-Masonry

#### II.

True knowledge, seated in the head,
Doth teach us Masons how to tread,
Doth teach &c.
   The paths we ought to go;
By which we ever friends create,
And drown all cares, strife, and debate,
And drown &c.
   Count none but fools our foe.

#### III.

Here sorrow knows not how to weep,
And watchful grief is lull'd to sleep,
And watchful &c.
   In our Lodge we know no care;
Join hand in hand before we part,
Each Brother take his glass with heart,
Each Brother &.
   And toast some charming fair.

#### VI.

Hear me, ye Gods, and whilst I live,
Good fellows and good liquor give,
Good fellows &c.
   Then always happy me;
Sometimes a gentle she I crave,
And when I'm summon'd to my grave,
And when &c.
   Adieu Free-Masonry.

PROLOGUES

# PROLOGUES and EPILOGUES.

## A PROLOGUE

*Spoken by Mr.* GRIFFITH *at the Theatre-Royal in* Dublin.

IF to delight, to humanize the mind,
The Savage World in social ties to bind;
To make the moral virtues all appear
Improv'd and useful, soften'd from severe.
  If these demand the tribute of our praise,
The teacher's honour, or the poet's lays.
How do we view 'em all compriz'd in thee,
Thrice honour'd, and mysterious Masonry.
  By thee erected, spacious domes arise,
And spires ascending glitter in the skies;
The wondrous whole, by heavenly art is crown'd,
And order in diversity is found.
  Thro' such a length of ages still how fair,
How bright, how blooming do thy looks appear?
And still shall bloom----Time, as it glides away,
Fears for its own, before thine shall decay.
  The use of accents from thy aid is thrown,
Thou form'st a silent language of thy own;
Disdain'st that records shou'd contain thy art,
And only liv'st within the faithful heart.
  Behold where kings, and a long shining train,
Of Garter'd Heroes wait upon thy reign,
And boast no honour but a Mason's name.
  Still in the dark let the unknowing stray,
No matter what they judge, or what they say:
Still may thy mystic secrets be conceal'd,
And only to a Brother be reveal'd.

## A PROLOGUE

As a wild rake that courts a virgin fair,
And tries in vain her virtue to infnare;
Tho' what he calls his heaven, he may obtain,
By putting on the matrimonial chain.
At length enrag'd to find fhe ftill is chafte,
Her modeft fame malicioufly would blaft:
So fome at our fraternity do rail,
Becaufe our Secrets we fo well conceal,
And curfe the centry with the flaming fword
That keeps Eve-droppers from the Mafon Word;
Tho', rightly introduc'd, all true men may
Obtain the fecret in a lawful way.
They'd have us counter to our honour run,
Do what they needs muft blame us for when done.
And when they find their teazing will not do,
Blinded with anger, heighth of folly fhow,
By railing at the thing they do not know.
   Not fo the affembly of the Scottifh Kirk,
Their wifdoms went a wifer way to work.
When they were told that Mafons practis'd charms,
Invok'd the Deel, and rais'd tempeftuous ftorms;
Two of their body prudently they fent
To learn what could by Mafonry be meant,
Admitted to the Lodge, and treated well,
At their return, the Affembly hop'd they'd tell.
" We fay nea mere, than this, (they both reply'd)
" Do what we've done, and ye'll be fatisfy'd"

---

## An EPILOGUE.

*Spoken by Mrs.* THURMOND, *a Mafon's Wife.*

With what malicious joy, e'er I knew better,
Have I been wont the Mafons to befpatter;
How greedily have I believ'd each lye
Contriv'd againft that fam'd Society?

*With*

With many more complain'd----'twas very hard
Women should from their Secrets be debarr'd,
When kings and statesmen to our sex reveal
Important business, which they should conceal:
That beauteous ladies, by their sparks ador'd,
Never could wheedle out the Masons word,
And oft their favours have bestow'd in vain,
Nor could one Secret for another gain.
I thought, unable to explain the matter,
Each Mason sure must be a woman-hater.
With sudden fear, and dismal horror struck,
I heard my spouse was to subscribe the book.
By all our loves I begg'd he would forbear,
Upon my knees I wept, and tore my hair;
But when I found him fixt, how I behav'd!
I thought him lost, and like a fury rav'd!
Believ'd he would for ever be undone,
By some strange operation undergone.

 When he came back, I found a change, 'tis true,
But such a change as did his Youth renew,
With rosie cheeks, and smiling grace he came,
And sparkling eyes, that spoke a bridegroom's flame.

 Ye married ladies, 'tis a happy life,
Believe me, that of a Free-Mason's wife,
Tho' they conceal the Secrets of their friends,
In love, and truth, they make us full amends.

---

## An EPILOGUE.

*Spoken by Mrs.* BELLAMY *at the Theatre-Royal in* Dublin.

WELL----here I'm come to let you know my thoughts,
Nay---ben't be alarm'd---I'll not attack your faults,
Alike be safe, the Cuckold, and the wit,
The Cuckold-maker, and the solemn Cit;
I'm in good humour, and am come to prattle,
Han't I a head well turn'd, d'ye think, to rattle;

But

But to clear up the point, and to be free,
What think you is my subject?----Masonry:
Tho' I'm afraid, as Lawyers cases clear,
My learn'd debate will leave you as you were;
But I'm a woman---and when I say that,
You know we'll talk---altho' we know not what.

What think you, ladies, 'ant it very hard,
That we should from this secret be debarr'd?
How comes it, that the softer hours of love,
To wheedle out this secret fruitless prove,
For we can wheedle when we hope to move:
What can it mean; why all this mighty pother,
These mystic signs, and solemn calling brother;
That we are quality'd in signs are known,
We can keep secrets too---but they're our own.

When my good man went first to be a Mason,
Tho' I resolv'd to put the smoother face on,
Yet, to speak truly, I began to fear
He must some dreadful operation bear:
But he return'd to satisfy each doubt,
And brought home every thing he carry'd out:
Nay, came improv'd, for on his face appear'd
A pleasing smile that every scruple clear'd,
Such added complaisance----so much good nature,
So much, so strangely alter'd for the better;
That to increase our mutual dear delight,
Wou'd he were made a Mason every night.

---

## An EPILOGUE.

*Spoken by Mrs.* HORTON *at the Theatre-Royal in* Drury-Lane, London.

WHERE are these Hydras? Let me vent my spleen;
Are these Free-Masons? Bless me, these are men!
And young, and brisk too; I expected monsters;
Brutes more prodigious than Italian songsters.

Lord!

( 40 )

Lord! how report will lye. How vain's this pother,
These look like sparks, who only love each other.
*[Ironicall*

Let easy faiths on such gross tales rely
'Tis false by rules of physiognomy;
I'll ne're believe it, poz, unless I try.
In proper time, and place, there's little doubt,
But one might find their wond'rous secrets out,
I shrewdly guess, egad, for all their shyness,
They'd render Signs, and Tokens too, of kindness,
If any truth in what I here observe is,
They'll quit ten Brothers for one Sister's service.

 But hold, wild fancy, whither art thou stray'd?
Where man's concern'd, alas, how frail is maid!
I come to storm, to scold, to rail, to rate;
And, see, the Accuser's turn'd the advocate!
Say, to what merits might not I pretend,
Who, tho' no sister, do yet prove your friend.
Wou'd beauty, thus, but in your cause appear,
'Twere something, Sirs, to be accepted----there.
*[Shews the Boxes.*

 Ladies, be gracious to the mystic arts
And kindly take the generous Masons parts;
Let no loquacious fop your joys partake,
He sues for telling, not for kissing's sake;
Firm to their trust the faithful Craft conceal,
They cry no roast-meat, fare they ne'er so well;
No tell-tale sneer shall raise the conscious Blush,
The loyal brother's Word is always----Hush.

 What tho' they quote old Solomon's decree,
And vainly boast, that thro' the world they're free,
With ease you'll humble the presumptuous braves,
One kind regard makes all these free men slaves.

*F I N I S.*